Letter to the Student

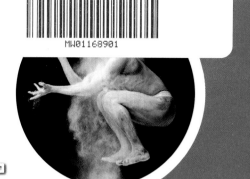

Dear Students and Faculty,

We are pleased to offer you this collection of con- temporary readings about psychology. All of the arti- cles in the collection originally appeared in our sister publications, SCIENTIFIC AMERICAN and SCIENTIFIC AMERICAN MIND. Some of the articles address the fundamental issues about psychology: How does the brain create consciousness and a sense of self? Why do we have emotions? How do drugs influence the mind? Other selections explore applications of psychology to per- sonal and social problems: How do we gain a sense of our own worth? How can we overcome psycho- logical disorders? Are there ways to protect ourselves from the stresses of life? What are the best techniques for helping people to be happier and healthier?

In selecting articles for this collection, we had several goals in mind. One was to bring to your attention some of the broad themes of psychology. Among the many articles published each year, a few stand out for capturing the fundamentals questions of the field. We include here articles on how emotional expres- sions such as crying evolved, on why infants don't use symbols to understand the world as adults do, and on how people sometimes form confident memories about events that in fact did not happen. Another goal that influenced our choice was to inform you of current findings of particular interest. These include a new review of what's known about drugs that may be able to enhance intelligence, an examination of recent techniques for overcoming stress that have been devel- oped to help soldiers returning from the war in Iraq, and a scientific detective story dispelling the myth that

we should always value high self-esteem in ourselves and in our children.

A third goal that led us to choose these articles was to illustrate how the scientific process really works. Textbooks can provide useful overviews of research findings, but they cannot adequately convey the excitement of the research process or the thought processes that led individual scientists to come up with the ideas underlying their investigations. While reading these articles, you'll have the opportunity to hear leading researchers not only explain their find- ings but also describe the background that led to their discoveries and how they generated and tested their ideas.

Our final goal was to present research that would com- plement the coverage in our textbook, *Psychology*. The order of the articles corresponds to the order in which the topics are covered in the book, and most chapters are accompanied by a relevant reading. Discussion Questions are included to focus students on the most salient information in each article. They can be used for essay assignments or to spark class- room discussion.

We hope you enjoy these wonderful SCIENTIFIC AMERICAN selections.

Daniel L. Schacter
Daniel T. Gilbert
Daniel M. Wegner

Contents

Contents

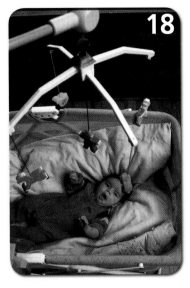

Contents

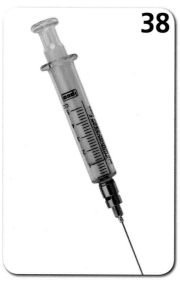

Contents

Contents

SCIENTIFIC
AMERICAN

Connecting with your customers is more than just good business...

it's a science.

Top marketers turn to Scientific American Custom Media to achieve their goals. Through award-winning[*] and highly-relevant content, Scientific American captivates key decision-makers in medicine, science, technology, business and public policy.

Whether you're positioning your brand as a thought leader or generating leads, Scientific American Custom Media will engage your audience with targeted publications, special sections, websites, podcasts, videos and events.

SCIENTIFIC AMERICAN CUSTOM MEDIA

For more information contact:
Lisa Pallatroni @ 212.451.8244
lpallatroni@SciAm.com

[*]Honored with the **2007 Media Award of Excellence** by the Friends of the National Institute of Dental and Craniofacial Research for the custom publication, "Oral and Whole Body Health"

THE NEUROBIOLOGY

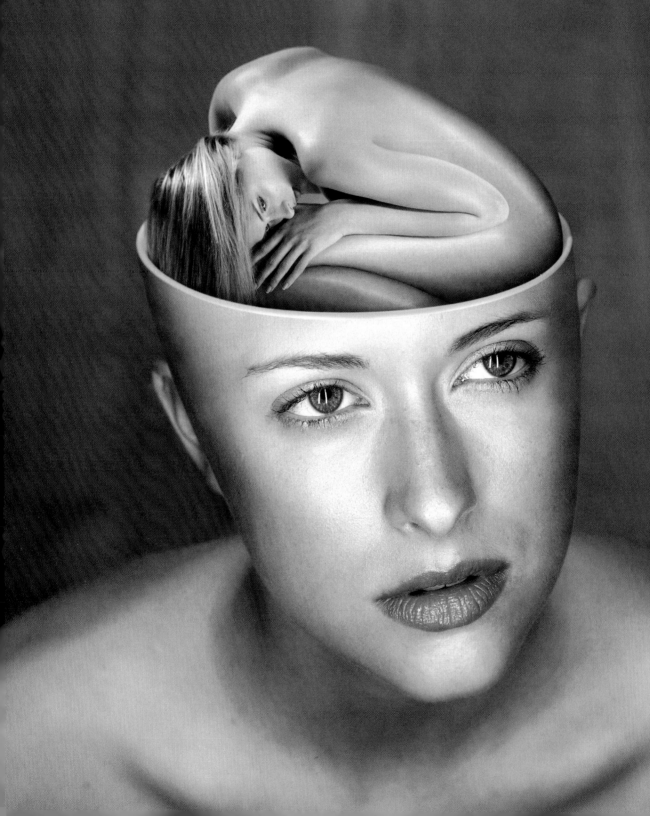

OF THE *Self*

Biologists are beginning to tease out how the brain gives rise to a constant sense of being oneself

The most obvious thing about yourself is your self. "You look down at your body and know it's yours," says Todd Heatherton, a psychologist at Dartmouth University. "You know it's your hand you're controlling when you reach out. When you have memories, you know that they are yours and not someone else's. When you wake up in the morning, you don't have to interrogate yourself for a long time about who you are."

The self may be obvious, but it is also an enigma. Heatherton himself shied away from direct study of it for years, even though he had been exploring self-control, self-esteem and other related issues since graduate school. "My interests were all around the self but not around the philosophical issue of what is the self," he explains. "I avoided speculations about what it means. Or I tried to, anyway."

Things have changed. Today Heatherton, along with a growing number of other scientists, is tackling this question head-on, seeking to figure out how the self emerges from the brain. In the past few years, they have begun to identify certain brain activities that may be essential for producing different aspects of self-awareness. They are now trying to determine how these activities give rise to the unified feeling we each have of being a single entity. This research is yielding clues to how the self may have evolved in our hominid ancestors. It may even help scientists treat Alzheimer's disease and other disorders that erode the knowledge of self and, in some cases, destroy it altogether.

By Carl Zimmer

The Self Is Special

AMERICAN PSYCHOLOGIST William James launched the modern study of this area in 1890 with his landmark book, *The Principles of Psychology.* "Let us begin with the Self in its widest acceptation, and follow it up to its most delicate and subtle form," he proposed. James argued that although the self might feel like a unitary thing, it has many facets—from awareness of one's own body to memories of oneself to the sense of where one fits into society. But James confessed to being baffled as to how the brain produced these self-related thoughts and wove them into a single ego.

Since then, scientists have found some telling clues through psychological experiments. Researchers interested in memories of the self, for instance, have asked volunteers questions about themselves, as well as about other people. Later the researchers gave the volunteers a pop quiz to see how well they remembered the questions. People consistently did a better job of remembering questions about themselves than about others. "When we tag things as relevant to the self, we remember them better," Heatherton says.

Some psychologists argued that these results simply meant that we are more familiar to ourselves than other people are to us. Some concluded instead that the self is special; the brain uses a different, more efficient system to process information about it. But psychological tests could not pick a winner from these competing explanations, because in many cases the hypotheses made the same predictions about experimental outcomes.

Further clues have emerged from injuries that affect some of the brain regions involved in the self. Perhaps the most famous case was that of Phineas Gage, a 19th-century railroad construction foreman who was standing in the

> The sight of someone being touched made her feel as if someone were touching her in the same place on her own body. She thought everyone had that experience.

wrong place at the wrong time when a dynamite blast sent a tamping iron through the air. It passed right through Gage's head, and yet, astonishingly, Gage survived.

Gage's friends, though, noticed something had changed. Before the accident, he had been considered an efficient worker and a shrewd businessman. Afterward he became profane, showed little respect for others and had a hard time settling on plans for the future. His friends said he was "no longer Gage."

Cases such as Gage's showed that the self is not the same as consciousness. People can have an impaired sense of themselves without being unconscious. Brain injuries have also revealed that the self is constructed in a complicated way. In 2002, for example, Stan B. Klein of the University of California at Santa Barbara and his colleagues reported on an amnesiac known as D.B. The man was 75 years old when he suffered brain damage from a heart attack and lost the ability to recall anything he had done or experienced before it. Klein tested D.B.'s

self-knowledge by giving him a list of 60 traits and asking him whether they applied to him somewhat, quite a bit, definitely, or not at all. Then Klein gave the same questionnaire to D.B.'s daughter and asked her to use it to describe her father. D.B.'s choices significantly correlated with his daughter's. Somehow D.B. had retained an awareness of himself without any access to memories of who he was.

Clues from Healthy Brains

IN RECENT YEARS, scientists have moved beyond injured brains to healthy ones, thanks to advances in brain imaging. At University College London, researchers have been using brain scans to decipher how we become aware of our own bodies. "This is the very basic, low-level first point of the self," UCL's Sarah-Jayne Blakemore says.

When our brains issue a command to move a part of our bodies, two signals are sent. One goes to the brain regions that control the particular parts of the body that need to move, and another goes to regions that monitor the movements. "I like to think of it as a 'cc' of an e-mail," Blakemore observes. "It's all the same information sent to a different place."

Our brains then use this copy to predict what kind of sensation the action will produce. A flick of an eye will make objects appear to move across our field of vision. Speaking will make us hear our own voice. Reaching for a doorknob will make us feel the cold touch of brass. If the actual sensation we receive does not closely match our prediction, our brains become aware of the difference. The mismatch may make us pay more attention to what we are doing or prompt us to adjust our actions to get the results we want.

Overview/*My Brain and Me*

- Increasing numbers of neurobiologists are exploring how the brain manages to form and maintain a sense of self.
- Several brain regions have been found to respond differently to information relating to the self than they do to information relating to others, even to very familiar others. For instance, such regions may be more active when people think about their own attributes than when they think about the characteristics of other individuals. These regions could be part of a self-network.
- For some, the goal of this research is to better understand, and to find new therapies for, dementia.

They recently showed a group of volunteers videos of other people being touched on the left or right side of the face or neck. The videos elicited the same responses in some areas of the volunteers' brains as occurred when the volunteers were touched on the corresponding parts of their own bodies. Blakemore was inspired to carry out the study when she met a 41-year-old woman, known as C., who took this empathy to a surprising extreme. The sight of someone being touched made C. feel as if someone were touching her in the same place on her own body. "She thought everyone had that experience," Blakemore remarks.

Blakemore scanned the woman's brain and compared its responses to those of normal volunteers. C.'s touch-sensitive regions reacted more strongly to the sight of someone else being touched than those regions did in the normal subjects. In addition, a site called the anterior insula (located on the brain's surface not far from the ear) became active in C. but not in the normal volunteers. Blakemore finds it telling that the anterior insula has also displayed activity in brain scans of people who are shown pictures of their own faces or who are identifying their own memories. It is possible that the anterior insula helps to designate some information as relating to ourselves instead of to other people. In the case of C., it simply assigns information incorrectly.

Brain scans have also shed light on other aspects of the self. Heatherton and his colleagues at Dartmouth have been using the technology to probe the mystery of why people remember information about themselves better than details about other people. They imaged the brains of volunteers who viewed a series of adjectives. In some cases, the researchers asked the subjects whether a word applied to the subjects themselves.

But if the sensation does not match our predictions at all, our brains interpret them as being caused by something other than ourselves. Blakemore and her colleagues documented this shift by scanning the brains of subjects they had hypnotized. When the researchers told the subjects their arms were being lifted by a rope and pulley, the subjects lifted their arms. But their brains responded as if someone else were lifting their arms, not themselves.

A similar lack of self-awareness may underlie certain symptoms of schizophrenia. Some schizophrenics become convinced that they cannot control their own bodies. "They reach over to grab a glass, and their movement is totally normal. But they say, 'It wasn't me. That machine over there controlled me and made me do it,'" Blakemore explains.

Studies on schizophrenics suggest that bad predictions of their own actions may be the source of these delusions. Because their sensations do not match their predictions, it feels as if something else is responsible. Bad predictions may also create the auditory hallucinations that some schizophrenics experience. Unable to predict the sound of their inner voice, they think it belongs to someone else.

One reason the sense of self can be so fragile may be that the human mind is continually trying to get inside the minds of other people. Scientists have discovered that so-called mirror neurons mimic the experiences of others. The sight of someone being painfully poked, for example, stimulates neurons in the pain region of our own brains. Blakemore and her colleagues have found that even seeing someone touched can activate mirror neurons.

THE AUTHOR

CARL ZIMMER is a journalist based in Connecticut. His latest book, *Soul Made Flesh: The Discovery of the Brain—and How It Changed the World,* was recently published in paperback. He also writes The Loom, a blog about biology (www.corante.com/loom/).

In others, they asked if a word applied to George W. Bush. In still other cases, they asked simply whether the word was shown in uppercase letters.

The researchers then compared the patterns of brain activity triggered by each kind of question. They found that questions about the self activated some regions of the brain that questions about someone else did not. Their results bolstered the "self is special" hypothesis over the "self is familiar" view.

A Common Denominator

ONE REGION that Heatherton's team found to be important to thinking about oneself was the medial prefrontal cortex, a patch of neurons located in the cleft between the hemispheres of the brain, directly behind the eyes. The same region has also drawn attention in studies on the self carried out by other laboratories. Heatherton is now trying to figure out what role it serves.

"It's ludicrous to think that there's any spot in the brain that's 'the self,' " he says. Instead he suspects that the area may bind together all the perceptions and memories that help to produce a sense of self, creating a unitary feeling of who we are. "Maybe it's something that brings information together in a meaningful way," Heatherton notes.

If he is right, the medial prefrontal cortex may play the same role for the self as the hippocampus plays in memory. The hippocampus is essential for forming new memories, but people can still retain old memories even after it is injured. Rather than storing information on its own, the hippocampus is believed to create memories by linking together far-flung parts of the brain.

The medial prefrontal cortex could be continuously stitching together a sense of who we are. Debra A. Gusnard of Washington University and her coworkers have investigated what occurs in the brain when it is at rest—that is, not engaged in any particular task. It turns out that the medial prefrontal cortex becomes more active at rest than during many kinds of thinking.

"Most of the time we daydream—we think about something that happened to us or what we think about other people. All this involves self-reflection," Heatherton says.

Other scientists are investigating the brain networks that may be organized by the medial prefrontal cortex. Matthew Lieberman of the University of California at Los Angeles has been using brain scans to solve the mystery of D.B., the man who knew himself even though he had amnesia. Lieberman and his colleagues scanned the brains of two sets of volunteers: soccer players and improvisational actors. The researchers then wrote up two lists of words, each of which was relevant to one of the groups. (Soccer players: athletic, strong, swift; actors: performer, dramatic, and so on.) They also composed a third list of words that did not apply specifically to either (messy and reliable, for example). Then they showed their subjects the words and asked them to decide whether

---

Just Another Pretty Face?

As Carl Zimmer notes in the accompanying article, investigators disagree over whether the brain treats the self as special—processing information about the self differently from information about other aspects of life. Some argue that parts of our brain that change their activity when we think about ourselves do so simply because we are familiar with ourselves, not specifically because the self is involved; anything else that was familiar would evoke the same response.

In one study addressing this question, researchers photographed a man referred to as J.W., whose right and left cerebral hemispheres operated independently as a result of surgery that had severed the connections (to treat intractable epilepsy). They also photographed someone very

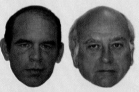

J.W.   Gazzaniga

familiar to the man—Michael Gazzaniga, a well-known brain researcher who had spent a lot of time with J.W. Next they created a series of images in which J.W.'s face morphed into Gazzaniga's (*below*) and displayed them in random order. For each image, they had J.W. answer the question "Is it me?" Then they repeated the process, having him answer, "Is it Mike?" They also performed the test with the faces of others well known to J.W.

They found that J.W.'s right hemisphere was more active when he recognized familiar others, but his left hemisphere was most active when he saw himself in the photographs. These findings lend support to the self-is-special hypothesis. The issue, though, is far from solved: both camps have evidence in their favor.   —*Ricki Rusting, managing editor*

90 percent J.W. ——————————————— Morphing ——————————————→ 10 percent J.W.

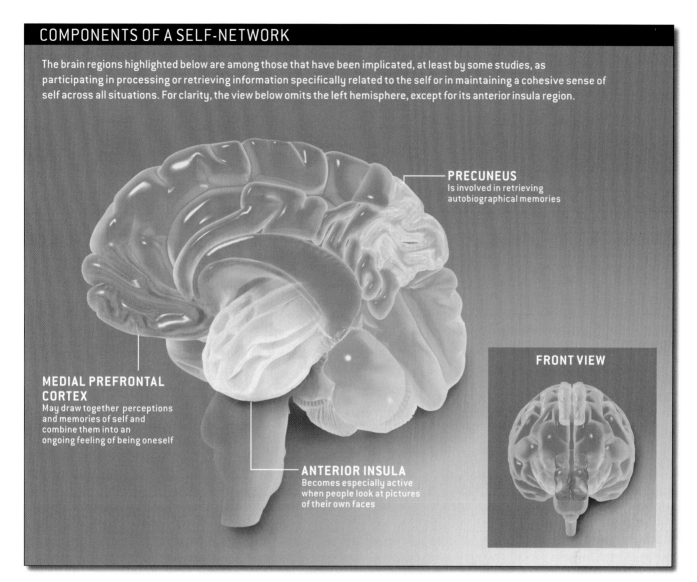
each one applied to themselves or not.

The volunteers' brains varied in their responses to the different words. Soccer-related words tended to increase activity in a distinctive network in the brains of soccer players, the same one that became more active in response to actor-related words in actors. When they were shown words related to the other group, a different network became more active. Lieberman refers to these two networks as the reflective system (or C system) and the reflexive system (or X system).

The C system taps into the hippocampus and other parts of the brain already known to retrieve memories. It also includes regions that can consciously hold pieces of information in mind. When we are in new circumstances, our sense of our self depends on think-ing explicitly about our experiences.

But Lieberman argues that over time, the X system takes over. Instead of memories, the X system encodes intuitions, tapping into regions that produce quick emotional responses based not on explicit reasoning but on statistical associations. The X system is slow to form its self-knowledge, because it needs many experiences to form these associations. But once it takes shape, it becomes very powerful. Soccer players know whether they are athletic, strong or swift without having to consult their memories. Those qualities are intimately wrapped up with who they are. On the other hand, they do not have the same gut instinct about whether they are dramatic, and in these cases they must think explicitly about their experi-ences. Lieberman's results may solve the mystery of D.B.'s paradoxical self-knowledge. It is conceivable that his brain damage wiped out his reflective system but not his reflexive system.

Although the neuroscience of the self is now something of a boom industry, it has its critics. "A lot of these studies aren't constrained, so they don't say anything," says Martha Farah, a cognitive neuroscientist at the University of Pennsylvania. The experiments, she argues, have not been designed carefully enough to eliminate other explanations—for example, that we use certain brain regions to think about any person, including ourselves. "I don't think there's any 'there' there," she says.

Heatherton and other scientists involved in this research think that Farah is being too tough on a young field. Still, they agree that they have yet to figure out much about the self-network and how it functions.

The Evolving Self

UNCOVERING THIS NETWORK may allow scientists to understand how our sense of self evolved. The primate ancestors of humans probably had the basic bodily self-awareness that is studied by Blakemore and her associates. (Studies on monkeys suggest that they make predictions about their own actions.) But humans have evolved a sense of self that is unparalleled in its complexity. It may be significant that the medial prefrontal cortex is "one of the most distinctly human brain regions," according to Lieberman. Not only is it larger in humans than in nonhuman primates, but it also has a greater concentration of uniquely shaped neurons called spindle cells. Scientists do not yet know what these neurons do but suspect that they play an important role in processing information. "It does seem like there's something special there," he comments.

Heatherton thinks that the human self-network may have evolved in response to the complex social life of our ancestors. For millions of years hominids lived in small bands, cooperating to find food and sharing what they found. "The only way that works is through self-control," he says. "You have to have cooperation, and you have to have trust." And these kinds of behaviors, he argues, require a sophisticated awareness of oneself.

If the full-fledged human self were a product of hominid society, that link would explain why there are so many tantalizing overlaps between how we think about ourselves and how we think about others. This overlap is not limited to the physical empathy that Blakemore studies. Humans are also uniquely skilled at inferring the intentions and thoughts of other members of their species. Scientists have scanned people engaged in using this so-called theory of mind, and some of the regions of the brain that become active are part of the network used in thinking about oneself

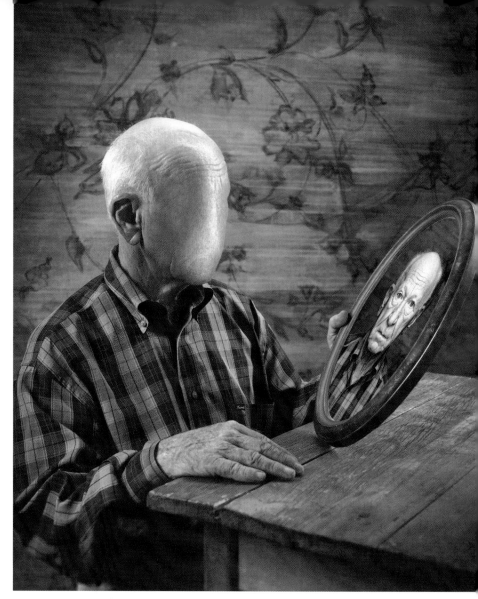

(including the medial prefrontal cortex). "Understanding ourselves and having a theory of mind are closely related," Heatherton says. "You need both to be a functioning human being."

The self requires time to develop fully. Psychologists have long recognized that it takes a while for children to acquire a stable sense of who they are. "They have conflicts in their self-concepts that don't bother them at all," Lieberman comments. "Little kids don't try to tell themselves, 'I'm still the same person.' They just don't seem to connect up the little pieces of the self-concept."

Lieberman and his colleagues wondered if they could track children's changing self-concept with brain imaging. They have begun studying a group of children and plan to scan them every 18 months from ages nine to 15. "We asked kids to think about themselves and to think about Harry Potter," he

says. He and his team have compared the brain activity in each task and compared the results with those in adults.

"When you look at 10-year-olds, they show this same medial prefrontal cortex activation as adults do," Lieberman notes. But another region that becomes active in adults, known as the precuneus, is a different story. "When they think about themselves, they activate this region *less* than they do when they think about Harry Potter."

Lieberman suspects that in children, the self-network is still coming online. "They've got the stuff, but they're not applying it like adults do."

Insights into Alzheimer's

ONCE THE SELF-NETWORK does come online, however, it works very hard. "Even with the visual system, I can close my eyes and give it something of a rest," comments William Seeley, a neurologist at the University of California, San Francisco. "But I can never get away from living in my body or representing the fact that I'm the same person I was 10 seconds or 10 years ago. I can never escape that, so that network must be busy."

One patient, described by Seeley and others in the journal *Neurology* in 2001, had collected jewelry and fine crystal for much of her life before abruptly starting to gather stuffed animals at age 62. A lifelong conservative, she began to berate people in stores who were buying

other dementia has destroyed a person's self. "Someone's going to say, 'Where's Gramps?'" he predicts. "And they're going to be able to take a picture of Gramps under certain conditions and say, 'Those circuits are not working.'"

Gazzaniga wonders whether people

> Someday a brain scan might determine whether dementia has destroyed a person's self. "Someone's going to say, 'Where's Gramps?' and they're going to be able to ... say, 'Those circuits are not working.'"

The more energy that a cell consumes, the greater its risk of damaging itself with toxic by-products. Seeley suspects that the hardworking neurons in the self-network are particularly vulnerable to this damage over the life span. Their vulnerability, he argues, may help neurologists make sense of some brain disorders that erode the self. "It is curious that we can't find certain pathological changes of Alzheimer's or other dementias in nonhuman species," Seeley says.

According to Seeley, the results of recent brain-imaging studies of the self agree with findings by him and others on people with Alzheimer's and other dementias. People with Alzheimer's develop tangled proteins in their neurons. Some of the first regions to be damaged are the hippocampus and precuneus, which are among the areas involved in autobiographical memories. "They help you bring images of your past and future into mind and play with them," Seeley notes. "People with Alzheimer's are just less able to move smoothly back and forth through time."

As agonizing as it may be for family members to watch a loved one succumb to Alzheimer's, other kinds of dementia can have even more drastic effects on the self. In a condition known as frontotemporal dementia, swaths of the frontal and temporal lobes degenerate. In many cases, the medial prefrontal cortex is damaged. As the disease begins to ravage the self-network, people may undergo strange changes in personality.

conservative books and declared that "Republicans should be taken off the earth." Other patients have suddenly converted to new religions or become obsessed with painting or photography. Yet they have little insight into why they are no longer their old selves. "They say pretty shallow things, like 'This is just the way I am now,'" Seeley says. Within a few years, frontotemporal dementia can lead to death.

Michael Gazzaniga, director of Dartmouth's Center for Cognitive Neuroscience and a member of the President's Council on Bioethics, believes that deciphering the self may pose a new kind of ethical challenge. "I think there's going to be the working out of the circuits of self—self-referential memory, self-description, personality, self-awareness," Gazzaniga says. "There's going to be a sense of what has to be in place for the self to be active."

It is even possible, Gazzaniga suggests, that someday a brain scan might determine whether Alzheimer's or some

will begin to consider the loss of the self when they write out their living wills. "Advanced directives will come into play," he predicts. "The issue will be whether you deliver health care. If people catch pneumonia, do you give them antibiotics or let them go?"

Seeley offers a more conservative forecast, arguing that a brain scan on its own probably will not change people's minds about life-and-death decisions. Seeley thinks the real value of the science of the self will come in treatments for Alzheimer's and other dementias. "Once we know which brain regions are involved in self-representation, I think we can take an even closer look at which cells in that brain region are important and then look deeper and say which molecules within cells and which genes that govern them lead to this vulnerability," he says. "And if we've done that, we've gotten closer to disease mechanisms and cures. That's the best reason to study all this. It's not just to inform philosophers." SA

MORE TO EXPLORE

A Self Less Ordinary: The Medial Prefrontal Cortex and You. C. Neil Macrae, Todd F. Heatherton and William M. Kelley in *Cognitive Neurosciences III*. Edited by Michael S. Gazzaniga. MIT Press, 2004.

Is Self Special? A Critical Review of Evidence from Experimental Psychology and Cognitive Neuroscience. Seth J. Gillihan and Martha J. Farah in *Psychological Bulletin*, Vol. 131, No. 1, pages 76–97; January 2005.

The Lost Self: Pathologies of the Brain and Identity. Edited by Todd E. Feinberg and Julian Paul Keenan. Oxford University Press, 2005.

Conflict and Habit: A Social Cognitive Neuroscience Approach to the Self. Matthew D. Lieberman and Naomi I. Eisenberger in *Psychological Perspectives on Self and Identity*, Vol. 4. Edited by A. Tesser, J. V. Wood and D. A. Stapel. American Psychological Association (in press). Available online at www.scn.ucla.edu/pdf/rt4053_c004Lieberman.pdf

Ambiguities and Perception

What uncertainty tells us about the brain
BY VILAYANUR S. RAMACHANDRAN AND DIANE ROGERS-RAMACHANDRAN

THE BRAIN abhors ambiguity, yet we are curiously attracted to it. Many famous visual illusions exploit ambiguity to titillate the senses. Resolving uncertainties creates a pleasant jolt in your brain, similar to the one you experience in the "Eureka!" moment of solving a problem. Such observations led German physicist, psychologist and ophthalmologist Hermann von Helmholtz to point out that perception has a good deal in common with intellectual problem solving. More recently, the idea has been revived and championed eloquently by neuropsychologist Richard L. Gregory of the University of Bristol in England.

So-called bistable figures, such as the mother-in-law/wife (a) and faces/vase (b) illusions, are often touted in textbooks as the prime example of how top-down influences (preexisting knowledge or expectations) from higher brain centers—where such perceptual tokens as "old" and "young" are encoded—can influence perception. Laypeople often take this to mean you can see anything you want to see, but this is nonsense—although, ironically, this view contains more truth than most of our colleagues would allow.

Fun Flips

Consider the simple case of the Necker cube (c and variation in d). You can view this illusion in one of two ways—either pointing up or pointing down. With a little practice, you can flip between these alternate percepts at

CURES

PHENYO-CAFFEIN

HEADACHE

MY GIRL & HER MOTHER
DO YOU SEE BOTH?

Copyrighted.

PHENYO-CAFFEIN CO.

will (still, it is great fun when it flips spontaneously; it feels like an amusing practical joke has been played on you). In fact, the drawing is compatible not only with two interpretations, as is commonly believed; there is actually an infinite set of trapezoidal shapes that can produce exactly the same retinal image, yet the brain homes in on a cube without hesitation. Note that at any time, you see only one or the other. The visual system appears to struggle to determine which of two cubes the drawing represents, but it has already solved the much larger perceptual problem by rejecting trillions of other configurations that could give rise to

the retinal pattern we call the Necker cube. Top-down attention and will, or intent, can only help you select between two percepts; you will not see any of the other possibilities no matter how hard you try.

Although the Necker cube is often used to illustrate the role of top-down influences, it, in fact, proves the very opposite—namely, that perception is generally immune to such influences. Indeed, if all perceptual computations mainly relied on top-down effects, they would be much too slow to help you in tasks related to survival and the propagation of your genes—escaping a predator, for example, or catching a meal or a mate.

It is important to recognize that ambiguity does not arise only in cleverly contrived displays such as on these two pages and in e, in which shading could make the circles appear to be convex or concave. In truth, ambiguity is the rule rather than the exception in perception; it is usually resolved by other co-

(It is great fun when it flips spontaneously; it feels like an **amusing practical joke** has been played on you.)

existing bottom-up (or sideways, if that is the right word) cues that exploit built-in statistical "knowledge" of the visual world. Such knowledge is wired into the neural circuitry of the visual system and deployed unconsciously to eliminate millions of false solutions. But the knowledge in question pertains to general properties of the world, not specific ones. The visual system has hardwired knowledge of surfaces, contours, depth, motion, illumination, and so on but not of umbrellas, chairs or dalmatians.

Motion Control

Ambiguity also arises in motion perception. In *f*, we begin with two light spots flashed simultaneously on diagonally opposite corners of an imaginary square, shown at *1*. The lights are then switched off and replaced by spots appearing on the remaining two corners, at *2*. The two frames are then cycled continuously. In this display, which we call a bistable quartet, the spots can be seen as oscillating vertically (*dashed arrows*) or horizontally (*solid arrows*) but never as both simultaneously—another example of ambiguity. It takes greater effort, but as with the cube, you can intentionally flip between these alternate percepts.

We asked ourselves what would happen if you scattered several such bistable-quartet stimuli on a computer screen. Would they all flip together when you mentally flipped one? Or, given that any one of them has a 50 percent chance of being vertical or horizontal, would each flip separately? That is, is the resolution of ambiguity global (all the quartets look the same), or does it occur piecemeal for different parts of the visual field?

The answer is clear: they all flip together. There must be global fieldlike effects in the resolution of ambiguity. You might want to try experimenting with this on your computer. You could also ask, Does the same rule apply for

the mother-in-law/wife illusion? How about the Necker cube? It is remarkable how much you can learn about perception using such simple displays; it is what makes the field so seductive.

We must be careful not to say that top-down influences play no role at all. In some of the figures, you can get stuck in one interpretation but can switch once you hear, verbally, that there is an alternative interpretation. It is as if your visual system—tapping into high-level memory—"projects" a template (for example, an old or young face) onto the fragments to facilitate their perception. One could argue that the recognition of *objects* can benefit from top-down processes that tap into attentional selection and memory. In contrast, seeing contours, surfaces, motion and depth is mainly from the bottom up (you can

"see" all the surfaces and corners of a cube and even reach out and grab it physically and yet not know or recognize it as a cube). In fact, we have both had the experience of peering at neurons all day through a microscope and then the next day "hallucinating" neurons everywhere: in trees, leaves and clouds. The extreme example of this effect is seen in patients who become

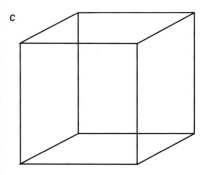

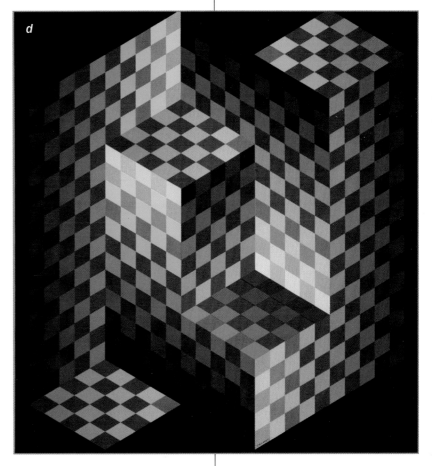

SCIENTIFIC AMERICAN MIND (c): VICTOR VASARELY, © ART RESOURCE, NEW YORK; PHOTOGRAPH BY ERICH LESSING, © 2007 ARTISTS RIGHTS SOCIETY, NEW YORK/ADAGP, PARIS (d)

(It is almost as though perception involves selecting **the one hallucination** that best matches sensory input.)

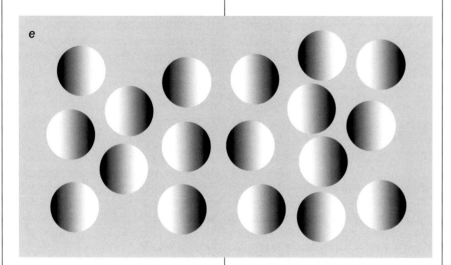

e

completely blind and start hallucinating elves, circus animals and other objects—called the Charles Bonnet syndrome. In these individuals, only top-down inputs contribute to perception—the bottom-up processes, missing because they are blind (from macular degeneration or cataracts), can no longer limit their hallucinations. It is almost as though we are all hallucinating all the time and what we call object perception merely involves *selecting* the one hallucination that best matches the current sensory input, however fragmentary. Vision, in short, is controlled hallucination.

But doesn't this statement contradict what we said earlier about vision being largely bottom-up? The answer to this riddle is "vision" is not a single process; perception of object*ness*—its outline, surface depth, and so on, as when you see a cube as cuboid—is largely bottom-up, whereas higher-level *identification* and categorization of objects into neurons or umbrellas do indeed benefit enormously from top-down memory-based influences.

How and What

Physiology also supports this distinction. Signals from the eyeballs are initially processed in the primary visual cortex at the back of the brain and then diverge into two visual pathways: the "how" pathway in the parietal lobe of the brain and the "what" pathway, linked to memories, in the temporal lobes. The former is concerned with spatial vision and navigation—reaching out to grab something, avoiding obstacles and pits, dodging missiles, and so on, none of which requires that you identify the object in question. The temporal lobes, on the other hand, enable you to recognize what an object actually is (pig, woman, table), and this process probably benefits partially from memory-based top-down effects. There are hybrid cases in which they overlap. For example, with the faces/vase illusion there is a bias to get stuck seeing the faces. But you can switch to seeing the vase without explicitly being told "look for the vase," if you are instead instructed to attend to the white region and see it as a foreground figure rather than as background.

Can the perception of ambiguous, bistable figures be biased in any way if they are preceded with other nonam-

biguous figures—a technique that is called priming? Priming has been explored extensively in linguistics (for instance, reading "foot" preceded by "leg" evokes the body part, but reading "foot" preceded by "inches" might suggest a ruler). Intriguingly, such priming can occur even if the first word appears too briefly to be seen consciously. Whether perception can be similarly primed has not been carefully studied. You might try it on friends.

f

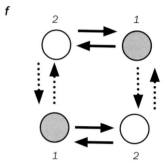

Finally, as we noted in one of our previous columns, you can construct displays that are always ambiguous, such as the devil's pitchfork or the perpetual staircase [see "Paradoxical Perceptions," April/May 2007]. Such paradoxical figures evoke wonder, delight and frustration at the same time—a microcosm of life itself. **M**

VILAYANUR S. RAMACHANDRAN and DIANE ROGERS-RAMACHANDRAN are at the Center for Brain and Cognition at the University of California, San Diego. They serve on *Scientific American Mind*'s board of advisers. The authors dedicate this column to Rama's mother, V. S. Meenakshi, who had an extremely quick, but not at all ambiguous, mind and who infinitely encouraged her son's curiosities.

(Further Reading)
- **The Intelligent Eye.** Richard L. Gregory. McGraw-Hill, 1970.
- **The Perception of Apparent Motion.** Vilayanur S. Ramachandran and Stuart M. Anstis in *Scientific American*, Vol. 254, No. 6, pages 102–109; June 1986.
- **A Critique of Pure Vision.** P. S. Churchland, V. S. Ramachandran and T. J. Sejnowski in *Large Scale Neuronal Theories of the Brain.* Edited by C. Koch and J. L. Davis. MIT Press, 1994.

SCIENTIFIC AMERICAN MIND

Paradoxical Perceptions

How does the brain sort out contradictory images?
BY VILAYANUR S. RAMACHANDRAN AND DIANE ROGERS-RAMACHANDRAN

PARADOXES—in which the same information may lead to two contradictory conclusions—give us pleasure and torment at the same time. They are a source of endless fascination and frustration, whether they involve philosophy (consider Russell's paradox, "This statement is false"), science—or perception. The Nobel Prize winner Peter Medawar once said that such puzzles have the same effect on a scientist or philosopher as the smell of burning rubber on an engineer: they create an irresistible urge to find the cause. As neuroscientists who study perception, we feel compelled to study the nature of visual paradoxes.

Let us take the simplest case. If different sources of information are not consistent with one another, what happens? Typically the brain will heed the one that is statistically more reliable and simply ignore the other source. For example, if you view the inside of a hollow mask from a distance, you will see the face as normal—that is, convex—even though your stereovision correctly signals that the mask is actually a hollow, concave face. In this case, your brain's cumulative experience with convex faces overrides and vetoes perception of the unusual occurrence of a hollow face.

Most tantalizing are the situations in which perception contradicts logic, leading to "impossible figures." British painter and printmaker William

Hogarth created perhaps the earliest such figure in the 18th century (*a*). A brief view of this image suggests nothing abnormal. Yet closer inspection reveals that it is logically impossible. Another example is the "devil's pitchfork," or Schuster's conundrum (*b*). Such impossible figures raise profound questions about the relation between perception and rationality.

In modern times, interest in such effects was partly revived by Swedish artist Oscar Reutersvärd. Known as the father of impossible figures, he devised numerous geometric paradoxes, including the "endless staircase" and the "impossible triangle." These two were also independently developed by Lionel and Roger Penrose, the famous father-and-son scientists, and *c* shows their version of what is now commonly called the Penrose triangle.

Dutch artist M. C. Escher playfully embedded such figures in his engravings exploring space and geometry. Consider Escher's staircase (*d*): no single part of the staircase is impossible or ambiguous, but the entire ensemble is logically impossible. You could be climbing the staircase upward forever and yet keep going in circles, never reaching the top. It epitomizes the human condition: we perpetually reach for perfection, never quite getting there!

Is this staircase truly a perceptual paradox? That is, is the brain unable to construct a coherent percept (or token of perception) because it has to simultaneously entertain two contradictory perceptions? We think not. Perception, almost by definition, has to be unified and stable at any given instant because

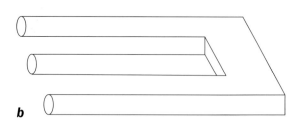

b

HISTORICAL PICTURE ARCHIVE *Corbis* (*a*); SCIENTIFIC AMERICAN MIND (*b*)

(If different sources of information are **not consistent** with one another, what happens?)

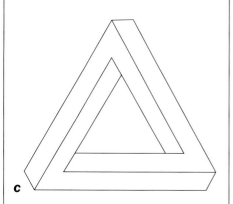

c

its whole purpose is to lead to an appropriate goal-directed action on our part. Indeed, some philosophers have referred to perception as "conditional readiness to act," which may seem like a bit of an overstatement.

Despite the common view that "we see what we believe," the perceptual mechanisms are really on autopilot as they compute and signal various aspects of the visual environment. You cannot choose to see what you want to see. (If I show you a blue lion, you see it as blue. You cannot say, "I will choose to see it as gold because it ought to be.") On the contrary, the paradox in *d* arises precisely because the perceptual mechanism performs a strictly local computation signaling "ascending stairs," whereas your conceptual/intellectual mechanism deduces that it is impossible logically for such an ascending staircase to form a closed loop. The goal of perception is to compute rapidly the approximate answers that are good enough for immediate survival; you cannot ruminate over whether the lion is near or far. The goal of rational conception—of logic—is to take time to produce a more accurate appraisal.

Genuine or Not?

Are impossible figures (aside from the triangle, to which we will return) genuine paradoxes within the domain of perception itself? One could argue that the perception itself remains, or

appears to remain, internally consistent, coherent and stable and that a genuinely paradoxical percept is an oxymoron. The staircase is no more a paradox than our seeing a visual illusion such as the Mueller-Lyer (*e*)—in which two lines of equal length appear to differ—but then measuring the two lines with a ruler and convincing ourselves at an intellectual level that the two lines are of identical length. The clash is between perception and intellect, not a genuine paradox within perception itself. On the other hand, "This statement is false" is a paradox entirely in the conceptual/linguistic realm.

Another compelling perception is the motion aftereffect. If you stare for a minute at stripes moving in one direction and then transfer your gaze to a stationary object, the object appears to move in the opposite direction that the stripes moved. This effect arises because your visual system has motion-detecting neurons signaling different directions, and the stripes constantly moving in one direction "fatigue" the neurons that would normally signal

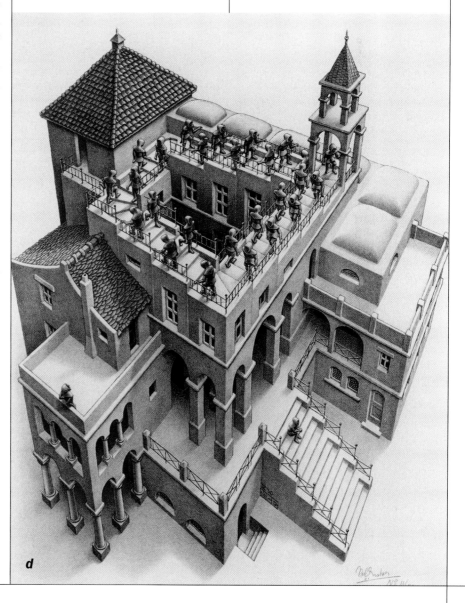

d

> (Perception is **virtually instantaneous**, whereas rational conception—logic—takes time.)

that direction [see "Stability of the Visual World," by Vilayanur S. Ramachandran and Diane Rogers-Ramachandran; SCIENTIFIC AMERICAN MIND, February/March 2006]. The result is a "rebound" that makes even stationary objects appear to move in the opposite direction.

Yet curiously, when you look at the object it seems to be moving in one direction, but it does not seem to get anywhere; it does not progress to a goal. This effect is often touted as a perceptual paradox: How can something appear to move but not change location? But once again, the percept itself is not paradoxical; rather it is signaling with certainty that the object is moving. It is your intellect that deduces it is not moving and infers a paradox.

Consider the much more familiar converse situation. You know (deduce) that the hour hand of your clock is moving, even though it looks stationary. It is not moving fast enough to excite motion-detecting neurons. Yet no one would call a clock hand's movement a paradox.

Perception-Cognition Boundary

There are borderline cases, as exemplified by the devil's pitchfork. In this display, some people can "see" the whole in a single glance. The local and global perceptual cues themselves are perceived as a single gestalt with internal contradictions. That is, one can apprehend the whole in a single glance and appreciate its paradoxical nature without thinking about it. Such dis-

plays remind us that despite the modular quasi-autonomous nature of perception and its apparent immunity from the intellect, the boundary between perception and cognition can blur.

The impossible triangle is similar. As shown by Richard L. Gregory, emeritus professor of neuropsychology at the University of Bristol in England, you can construct a complicated 3-D object (*f*) that would produce the image in *g* only when viewed from one particular vantage point. From that specific angle, the object appears to be a triangle confined to a single plane. But your perception rejects such highly improbable events, even when your intellect is convinced of their possibility (after being shown the view at *g*). Thus, even when you understand conceptually the unusual shape of object *f*, you continue to see a closed triangle when viewing *g*, rather than the object (*f*) that actually gives rise to it.

How would one test these notions empirically? With the Escher staircase, one could exploit the fact that perception is virtually instantaneous, whereas cogitation takes time. One could present the display briefly—a

short enough time to prevent cognition from kicking in—say, a tenth of a second followed by a masking stimulus (which prevents continued visual processing after removal of the test figure). The prediction would be that the picture should no longer look paradoxical unless the stimulus duration were lengthened adequately. The same could be tried for the devil's pitchfork, which is more likely to be a genuine perceptual paradox. In this case, the mask may not be able to "dissect" it into two distinct (perception or cognition) stages. It may boil down to a matter of scale or complexity.

Whatever paradoxes' origins, no one can fail to be intrigued by these enigmatic displays. They perpetually titillate our senses and challenge all our notions of reality and illusion. Human life, it would seem, is delightfully bedeviled by paradox. M

VILAYANUR S. RAMACHANDRAN and DIANE ROGERS-RAMACHANDRAN are at the Center for Brain and Cognition at the University of California, San Diego. They serve on *Scientific American Mind*'s board of advisers.

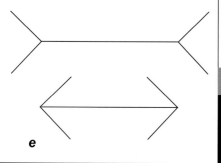

e

(Further Reading)

◆ **A New Ambiguous Figure: A Three-Stick Clovis.** D. H. Schuster in *American Journal of Psychology,* Vol. 77, page 673; 1964.
◆ **The Intelligent Eye.** Richard L. Gregory. McGraw Hill, 1970.
◆ More ambiguous figures are available at **im-possible.info/english/art/index.html**

SCIENTIFIC AMERICAN MIND (e); COURTESY OF RICHARD L. GREGORY *University of Bristol* (f and g)

Creating False Memories

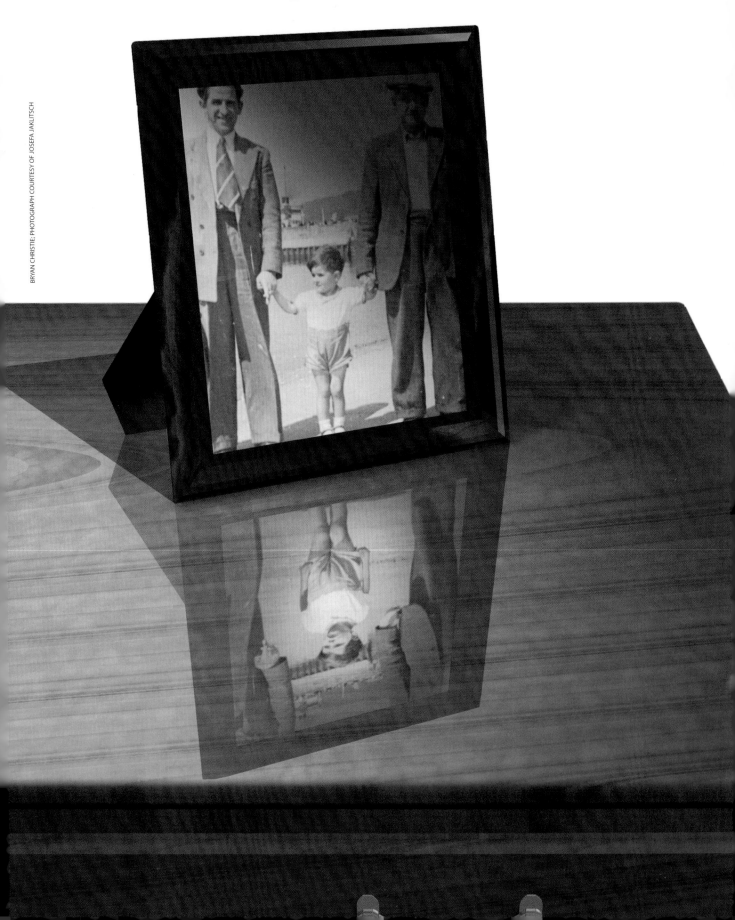

Researchers are showing how suggestion and imagination can create "memories" of events that did not actually occur

by Elizabeth F. Loftus

In 1986 Nadean Cool, a nurse's aide in Wisconsin, sought therapy from a psychiatrist to help her cope with her reaction to a traumatic event experienced by her daughter. During therapy, the psychiatrist used hypnosis and other suggestive techniques to dig out buried memories of abuse that Cool herself had allegedly experienced. In the process, Cool became convinced that she had repressed memories of having been in a satanic cult, of eating babies, of being raped, of having sex with animals and of being forced to watch the murder of her eight-year-old friend. She came to believe that she had more than 120 personalities—children, adults, angels and even a duck—all because, Cool was told, she had experienced severe childhood sexual and physical abuse. The psychiatrist also performed exorcisms on her, one of which lasted for five hours and included the sprinkling of holy water and screams for Satan to leave Cool's body.

When Cool finally realized that false memories had been planted, she sued the psychiatrist for malpractice. In March 1997, after five weeks of trial, her case was settled out of court for $2.4 million.

Nadean Cool is not the only patient to develop false memories as a result of questionable therapy. In Missouri in 1992 a church counselor helped Beth Rutherford to remember during therapy that her father, a clergyman, had regularly raped her between the ages of seven and 14 and that her mother sometimes helped him by holding her down. Under her therapist's guidance, Rutherford developed memories of her father twice impregnating her and forcing her to abort the fetus herself with a coat hanger. The father

had to resign from his post as a clergyman when the allegations were made public. Later medical examination of the daughter revealed, however, that she was still a virgin at age 22 and had never been pregnant. The daughter sued the therapist and received a $1-million settlement in 1996.

About a year earlier two juries returned verdicts against a Minnesota psychiatrist accused of planting false memories by former patients Vynnette Hamanne and Elizabeth Carlson, who under hypnosis and sodium amytal, and after being fed misinformation about the workings of memory, had come to remember horrific abuse by family members. The juries awarded Hammane $2.67 million and Carlson $2.5 million for their ordeals.

In all four cases, the women developed memories about childhood abuse in therapy and then later denied their authenticity. How can we determine if memories of childhood abuse are true or false? Without corroboration, it is very difficult to differentiate between false memories and true ones. Also, in these cases, some memories were contrary to physical evidence, such as explicit and detailed recollections of rape and abortion when medical examination confirmed virginity. How is it possible for people to acquire elaborate and confident false memories? A growing number of investigations demonstrate that under the right circumstances false memories can be instilled rather easily in some people.

My own research into memory distortion goes back to the early 1970s, when I began studies of the "misinformation effect." These studies show that when people who witness an event are later exposed to new and misleading information about it, their recollections often become distorted. In one example, participants viewed a simulated automobile accident at an intersection with

a stop sign. After the viewing, half the participants received a suggestion that the traffic sign was a yield sign. When asked later what traffic sign they remembered seeing at the intersection, those who had been given the suggestion tended to claim that they had seen a yield sign. Those who had not received the phony information were much more accurate in their recollection of the traffic sign.

My students and I have now conducted more than 200 experiments involving over 20,000 individuals that document how exposure to misinformation induces memory distortion. In these studies, people "recalled" a conspicuous barn in a bucolic scene that contained no buildings at all, broken glass and tape recorders that were not in the scenes they viewed, a white instead of a blue vehicle in a crime scene, and Minnie Mouse when they actually saw Mickey Mouse. Taken together, these studies show that misinformation can change an individual's recollection in predictable and sometimes very powerful ways.

Misinformation has the potential for invading our memories when we talk to other people, when we are suggestively interrogated or when we read or view media coverage about some event that we may have experienced ourselves. After more than two decades of exploring the power of misinformation, researchers have learned a great deal about the conditions that make people susceptible to memory modification. Memories are more easily modified, for instance, when the passage of time allows the original memory to fade.

False Childhood Memories

It is one thing to change a detail or two in an otherwise intact memory but quite another to plant a false memory of an event that never happened. To study false memory, my students and I

FALSE MEMORIES are often created by combining actual memories with suggestions received from others. The memory of a happy childhood outing to the beach with father and grandfather, for instance, can be distorted by a suggestion, perhaps from a relative, into a memory of being afraid or lost. False memories also can be induced when a person is encouraged to imagine experiencing specific events without worrying about whether they really happened or not.

first had to find a way to plant a pseudo-memory that would not cause our subjects undue emotional stress, either in the process of creating the false memory or when we revealed that they had been intentionally deceived. Yet we wanted to try to plant a memory that would be at least mildly traumatic, had the experience actually happened.

My research associate, Jacqueline E. Pickrell, and I settled on trying to plant a specific memory of being lost in a shopping mall or large department store at about the age of five. Here's how we did it. We asked our subjects, 24 individuals ranging in age from 18 to 53, to try to remember childhood events that had been recounted to us by a parent, an older sibling or another close relative. We prepared a booklet for each participant containing one-paragraph stories about three events that had actually happened to him or her and one that had not. We constructed the false event using information about a plausible shopping trip provided by a relative, who also verified that the participant had not in fact been lost at about the age of five. The lost-in-the-mall scenario included the following elements: lost for an extended period, crying, aid and comfort by an elderly woman and, finally, reunion with the family.

After reading each story in the book-

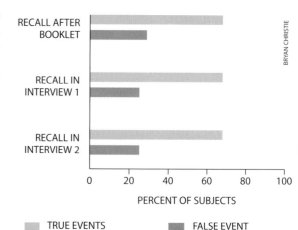

let, the participants wrote what they remembered about the event. If they did not remember it, they were instructed to write, "I do not remember this." In two follow-up interviews, we told the participants that we were interested in examining how much detail they could remember and how their memories compared with those of their relative. The event paragraphs were not read to them verbatim, but rather parts were provided as retrieval cues. The participants recalled something about 49 of the 72 true events (68 percent) immediately after the initial reading of the booklet and also in each of the two follow-up interviews. After reading the booklet, seven of the 24 participants (29 percent) remembered either partially or fully the false event constructed for them, and in the two follow-up interviews six participants (25 percent) continued to claim that they remembered the fictitious event. Statistically, there were some differences between the true memories and the false ones: participants used more words to describe the true memories, and they rated the true memories as being somewhat more clear. But if an onlooker were to ob-

serve many of our participants describe an event, it would be difficult indeed to tell whether the account was of a true or a false memory.

Of course, being lost, however frightening, is not the same as being abused. But the lost-in-the-mall study is not about real experiences of being lost; it is about planting false memories of being lost. The paradigm shows a way of instilling false memories and takes a step toward allowing us to understand how this might happen in real-world settings. Moreover, the study provides evidence that people can be led to remember their past in different ways, and they can

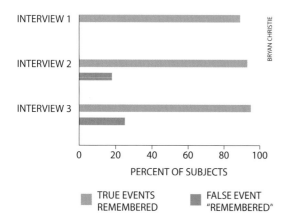

RECALL OF PLANTED CHILDHOOD EVENTS in this study appears to increase slightly after the details become familiar to the subject and the source of the information is forgotten. Ira Hyman and his colleagues at Western Washington University presented subjects with true events provided by relatives along with a false event—such as spilling a punch bowl on the parents of the bride at a wedding. None of the participants remembered the false event when first told about it, but in two follow-up interviews, initially 18 percent and later 25 percent of the subjects said they remembered something about the incident.

FALSE MEMORY TOOK ROOT in roughly 25 percent of the subjects in this study by the author and her co-workers. The study was designed to create a false recollection of being lost at age five on a shopping trip. A booklet prepared for each participant included the false event and three events that he or she had actually experienced. After reading the scenarios, 29 percent of the subjects "recalled" something about being lost in the mall. Follow-up interviews showed there was little variation over time in recalling both the false and true events.

even be coaxed into "remembering" entire events that never happened.

Studies in other laboratories using a similar experimental procedure have produced similar results. For instance, Ira Hyman, Troy H. Husband and F. James Billing of Western Washington University asked college students to recall childhood experiences that had been recounted by their parents. The researchers told the students that the study was about how people remember shared experiences differently. In addition to actual events reported by parents, each participant was given one false event—either an overnight hospitalization for a high fever and a possible ear infection, or a birthday party with pizza and a clown—that supposedly happened at about the age of five. The parents confirmed that neither of these events actually took place.

Hyman found that students fully or partially recalled 84 percent of the true events in the first interview and 88 percent in the second interview. None of the participants recalled the false event during the first interview, but 20 percent said they remembered something about the false event in the second interview. One participant who had been exposed to the emergency hospitalization story later remembered a male doctor, a female nurse and a friend from church who came to visit at the hospital.

In another study, along with true events Hyman presented different false events, such as accidentally spilling a bowl of punch on the parents of the bride at a wedding reception or having to evacuate a grocery store when the overhead sprinkler systems erroneously activated. Again, none of the participants recalled the false event during the first interview, but 18 percent remembered something about it in the second interview and 25 percent in the third interview. For example, during the first interview, one participant, when asked about the fictitious wedding event, stated, "I have no clue. I have never heard that one before." In the second interview, the participant said, "It was an outdoor wedding, and I think we were running around and knocked something over like the punch bowl or something and made a big mess and of course got yelled at for it."

Imagination Inflation

The finding that an external suggestion can lead to the construction of false childhood memories helps us understand the process by which false memories arise. It is natural to wonder whether this research is applicable in real situations such as being interrogated by law officers or in psychotherapy. Although strong suggestion may not routinely occur in police questioning or therapy, suggestion in the form of an imagination exercise sometimes does. For instance, when trying to obtain a confession, law officers may ask a suspect to imagine having participated in a criminal act. Some mental health professionals encourage patients to imagine childhood events as a way of recovering supposedly hidden memories.

Surveys of clinical psychologists reveal that 11 percent instruct their clients to "let the imagination run wild," and 22 percent tell their clients to "give free rein to the imagination." Therapist Wendy Maltz, author of a popular book on childhood sexual abuse, advocates telling the patient: "Spend time imagin-

JASON GOLTZ

ing that you were sexually abused, without worrying about accuracy, proving anything, or having your ideas make sense.... Ask yourself...these questions: What time of day is it? Where are you? Indoors or outdoors? What kind of things are happening? Is there one or more person with you?" Maltz further recommends that therapists continue to ask questions such as "Who would have been likely perpetrators? When were you most vulnerable to sexual abuse in your life?"

The increasing use of such imagination exercises led me and several colleagues to wonder about their consequences. What happens when people imagine childhood experiences that did not happen to them? Does imagining a childhood event increase confidence that it occurred? To explore this, we designed a three-stage procedure. We first asked individuals to indicate the likelihood that certain events happened to them during their childhood. The list contains 40 events, each rated on a scale ranging from "definitely did not happen" to "definitely did happen." Two weeks later we asked the participants to imagine that they had experienced some of these events. Different subjects were asked to imagine different events. Sometime later the participants again were asked to respond to the original list of 40 childhood events, indicating how likely it was that these events actually happened to them.

Consider one of the imagination exercises. Participants are told to imagine playing inside at home after school, hearing a strange noise outside, running toward the window, tripping, falling, reaching out and breaking the window with their hand. In addition, we asked participants questions such as "What did you trip on? How did you feel?"

In one study 24 percent of the participants who imagined the broken-window scenario later reported an increase in confidence that the event had occurred, whereas only 12 percent of those who were not asked to imagine the incident reported an increase in the likelihood that it had taken place. We found this "imagination inflation" effect in each of the eight events that participants were asked to imagine. A number of possible explanations come to mind. An obvious one is that an act of imagination simply makes the event seem more familiar and that familiarity is mistakenly related to childhood memories rather than to the act of imagination. Such source confusion—when a person does not remember the source of information—can be especially acute for the distant experiences of childhood.

Studies by Lyn Goff and Henry L. Roediger III of Washington University of recent rather than childhood experiences more directly connect imagined actions to the construction of false memory. During the initial session, the researchers instructed participants to perform the stated action, imagine doing it or just listen to the statement and do nothing else. The actions were simple ones: knock on the table, lift the stapler, break the toothpick, cross your fingers, roll your eyes. During the second session, the participants were asked to imagine some of the actions that they had not previously performed. During the final session, they answered questions about what actions they actually performed during the initial session. The investigators found that the more times participants imagined an unperformed action, the more likely they were to remember having performed it.

Impossible Memories

It is highly unlikely that an adult can recall genuine episodic memories from the first year of life, in part because the hippocampus, which plays a key role in the creation of memories, has not matured enough to form and store long-lasting memories that can be retrieved in adulthood. A procedure for planting "impossible" memories about experiences that occur shortly after birth has been developed by the late Nicholas Spanos and his collaborators at Carleton University. Individuals are led to believe that they have well-coordinated eye movements and visual exploration skills probably because they were born in hospitals that hung swinging, colored mobiles over infant cribs. To confirm whether they had such an experience, half the participants are hypnotized, age-regressed to the day after birth and asked what they remembered. The other half of the group participates in a "guided mnemonic restructuring" procedure that uses age regression as well as active encouragement to re-create the infant experiences by imagining them.

Spanos and his co-workers found that the vast majority of their subjects were susceptible to these memory-planting procedures. Both the hypnotic and guided participants reported infant memories. Surprisingly, the guided group did so somewhat more (95 versus 70 percent). Both groups remembered the colored mobile at a relatively high rate (56 percent of the guided group and 46 percent of the hypnotic subjects). Many participants who did not remember the

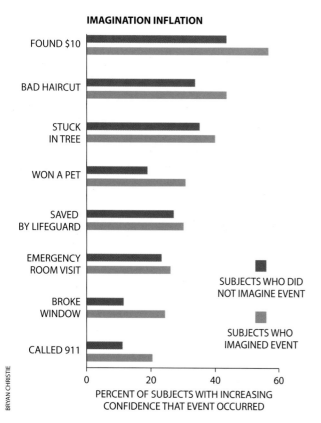

IMAGINATION INFLATION

FOUND $10
BAD HAIRCUT
STUCK IN TREE
WON A PET
SAVED BY LIFEGUARD
EMERGENCY ROOM VISIT
BROKE WINDOW
CALLED 911

SUBJECTS WHO DID NOT IMAGINE EVENT

SUBJECTS WHO IMAGINED EVENT

0   20   40   60
PERCENT OF SUBJECTS WITH INCREASING CONFIDENCE THAT EVENT OCCURRED

IMAGINING AN EVENT can increase a person's belief that the fictitious event actually happened. To study the "imagination inflation" effect, the author and her colleagues asked participants to indicate on a scale the likelihood that each of 40 events occurred during their childhood. Two weeks later they were given guidance in imagining some of the events they said had not taken place and then were asked to rate the original 40 events again. Whereas all participants showed increased confidence that the events had occurred, those who took part in actively imagining the events reported an even greater increase.

Creating False Memories

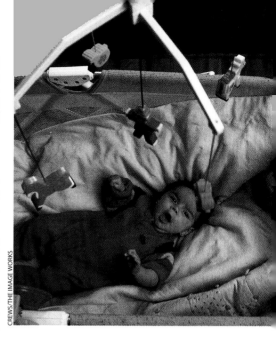

MEMORIES OF INFANCY—such as a mobile hanging over a crib—can be induced even though it is highly unlikely that events from the first year of life can be recalled. In a study by the late Nicholas Spanos and his colleagues at Carleton University, "impossible" memories of the first day of life were planted using either hypnosis or a guided mnemonic restructuring procedure. The mobile was "remembered" by 46 percent of the hypnotized group and by 56 percent of the guided group.

mobile did recall other things, such as doctors, nurses, bright lights, cribs and masks. Also, in both groups, of those who reported memories of infancy, 49 percent felt that they were real memories, as opposed to 16 percent who claimed that they were merely fantasies. These findings confirm earlier studies that many individuals can be led to construct complex, vivid and detailed false memories via a rather simple procedure. Hypnosis clearly is not necessary.

How False Memories Form

In the lost-in-the-mall study, implantation of false memory occurred when another person, usually a family member, claimed that the incident happened. Corroboration of an event by another person can be a powerful technique for instilling a false memory. In fact, merely claiming to have seen a person do something can lead that person to make a false confession of wrongdoing.

This effect was demonstrated in a study by Saul M. Kassin and his colleagues at Williams College, who investigated the reactions of individuals falsely accused of damaging a computer by pressing the wrong key. The innocent participants initially denied the charge, but when a confederate said that she had seen them perform the action, many participants signed a confession, internalized guilt for the act and went on to confabulate details that were consistent with that belief. These findings show that false incriminating evidence can induce people to accept guilt for a crime they did not commit and even to develop memories to support their guilty feelings.

Research is beginning to give us an understanding of how false memories of complete, emotional and self-participatory experiences are created in adults. First, there are social demands on individuals to remember; for instance, researchers exert some pressure on participants in a study to come up with memories. Second, memory construction by imagining events can be explicitly encouraged when people are having trouble remembering. And, finally, individuals can be encouraged not to think about whether their constructions are real or not. Creation of false memories is most likely to occur when these external factors are present, whether in an experimental setting, in a therapeutic setting or during everyday activities.

False memories are constructed by combining actual memories with the content of suggestions received from others. During the process, individuals may forget the source of the information. This is a classic example of source confusion, in which the content and the source become dissociated.

Of course, because we can implant false childhood memories in some individuals in no way implies that all memories that arise after suggestion are necessarily false. Put another way, although experimental work on the creation of false memories may raise doubt about the validity of long-buried memories, such as repeated trauma, it in no way disproves them. Without corroboration, there is little that can be done to help even the most experienced evaluator to differentiate true memories from ones that were suggestively planted.

The precise mechanisms by which such false memories are constructed await further research. We still have much to learn about the degree of confidence and the characteristics of false memories created in these ways, and we need to discover what types of individuals are particularly susceptible to these forms of suggestion and who is resistant.

As we continue this work, it is important to heed the cautionary tale in the data we have already obtained: mental health professionals and others must be aware of how greatly they can influence the recollection of events and of the urgent need for maintaining restraint in situations in which imagination is used as an aid in recovering presumably lost memories. **SA**

The Author

ELIZABETH F. LOFTUS is professor of psychology and adjunct professor of law at the University of Washington. She received her Ph.D. in psychology from Stanford University in 1970. Her research has focused on human memory, eyewitness testimony and courtroom procedure. Loftus has published 18 books and more than 250 scientific articles and has served as an expert witness or consultant in hundreds of trials, including the McMartin preschool molestation case. Her book *Eyewitness Testimony* won a National Media Award from the American Psychological Foundation. She has received honorary doctorates from Miami University, Leiden University and John Jay College of Criminal Justice. Loftus was recently elected president of the American Psychological Society.

Further Reading

THE MYTH OF REPRESSED MEMORY. Elizabeth F. Loftus and Katherine Ketcham. St. Martin's Press, 1994.
THE SOCIAL PSYCHOLOGY OF FALSE CONFESSIONS: COMPLIANCE, INTERNALIZATION, AND CONFABULATION. Saul M. Kassin and Katherine L. Kiechel in *Psychological Science*, Vol. 7, No. 3, pages 125–128; May 1996.
IMAGINATION INFLATION: IMAGINING A CHILDHOOD EVENT INFLATES CONFIDENCE THAT IT OCCURRED. Maryanne Garry, Charles G. Manning, Elizabeth F. Loftus and Steven J. Sherman in *Psychonomic Bulletin and Review*, Vol. 3, No. 2, pages 208–214; June 1996.
REMEMBERING OUR PAST: STUDIES IN AUTOBIOGRAPHICAL MEMORY. Edited by David C. Rubin. Cambridge University Press, 1996.
SEARCHING FOR MEMORY: THE BRAIN, THE MIND, AND THE PAST. Daniel L. Schacter. BasicBooks, 1996.

JUMPING TO CONCLUSIONS

Can people be counted on to make sound judgments?

By
Deanna
Kuhn

A four-year-old watches as a monkey hand puppet approaches a vase containing a red and a blue plastic flower. The monkey sneezes. The monkey backs away, returns to sniff again, and again sneezes. An adult then removes the red flower and replaces it with a yellow one. The monkey comes up to smell the yellow and blue flowers twice and each time sneezes. The adult next replaces the blue flower with the red one. The monkey comes up to smell the red and yellow flowers and this time does not sneeze.

The child is then asked, "Can you give me the flower that makes Monkey sneeze?" When psychologists Laura E. Schulz and Alison Gopnik, both then at the University of California, Berkeley, did this experiment, 79 percent of four-year-olds correctly chose the blue flower. As their research makes clear, even very young children have begun to understand cause and effect. This process is critical to their ability to make sense of their world and to make their way in it.

With such powers of discernment already in place by age four, people should be highly skilled at identifying cause and effect—causal reasoning—by the time they are adults, shouldn't they? Indeed, a substantial body of contemporary research suggests that is the case, highlighting the nuanced judgments adults are capable of—such as making consistent estimates, across different circumstances, of the numerical probabilities that two events are causally related.

Here I present some evidence that gives a very different impression: the everyday causal reasoning of the average adult regarding familiar topics appears highly fallible. People connect two events as cause and effect based on little or no evidence, and they act on these judgments—they jump to conclusions. By learning more about precisely how they do so, researchers can develop ways to improve thinking. Such efforts could help educators in their mission to inspire solid, careful thinking in young minds.

A possible explanation for the discrepancy between our findings and much of the relevant literature is that researchers studying

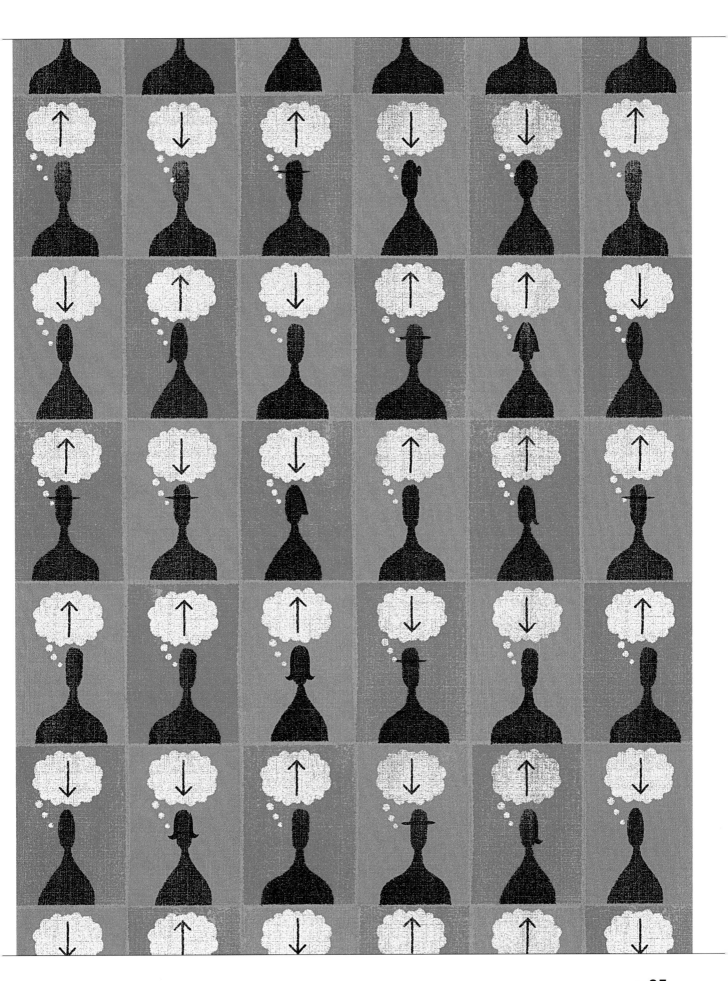

Case Studies in Cause and Effect

Do door prizes work?

In a study, adults had difficulty judging which factors yielded the best performance at fund-raising parties. The results provided (*below*) showed a causal relation between "auction" and sales (compare first and third parties) and no causal relation between "comedian" and sales (compare second and third). Information was insufficient to determine other feature effects. Yet 83 percent of the volunteers said two or more features increased sales, and 45 percent claimed three or all four did so. Most also reported feeling certain about the correctness of their (often erroneous) judgments.

First party	Second party	Third party
• Door prizes	• Door prizes	• Door prizes
• Comedian	• Auction	• Auction
• Costumes	• Costumes	• Comedian
		• Costumes
SALES: MEDIUM	**SALES: HIGH**	**SALES: HIGH**

A second reasoning task asked volunteers to make predictions, all of which were indeterminate (because the effects of door prizes and costumes were unknown). Respondents displayed inconsistent logic. Particularly difficult for them was recognizing that a feature whose presence had a positive influence on an outcome would negatively affect the outcome when it was removed. For example, in the prediction question involving door prizes and a comedian (*lower left*), only 40 percent of respondents circled the absence of an auction as affecting the outcome, although 85 percent had correctly labeled it as causal. As before, people were nonetheless certain about their judgments. —*D.K.*

- **Door prizes**   •**Auction**
- **Comedian**

SALES: LOW   MEDIUM   HIGH

How certain are you? (circle one)

Very certain   Certain
Think so but not certain   Just guessing

Which influenced your prediction?
(circle as many as apply)
- Door prizes
- Auction
- Comedian
- Absence of costumes

- **Auction**   • **Costumes**
- **Comedian**

SALES: LOW   MEDIUM   HIGH

How certain are you? (circle one)

Very certain   Certain
Think so but not certain   Just guessing

Which influenced your prediction?
(circle as many as apply)
- Auction
- Costumes
- Comedian
- Absence of door prizes

- **Door prizes**
- **Comedian**

SALES: LOW   MEDIUM   HIGH

How certain are you? (circle one)

Very certain   Certain
Think so but not certain   Just guessing

Which influenced your prediction?
(circle as many as apply)
- Door prizes
- Comedian
- Absence of auction
- Absence of costumes

- **Auction**
- **Costumes**

SALES: LOW   MEDIUM   HIGH

How certain are you? (circle one)

Very certain   Certain
Think so but not certain   Just guessing

Which influenced your prediction?
(circle as many as apply)
- Auction
- Costumes
- Absence of comedian
- Absence of door prizes

causal reasoning skills in adults have typically based their conclusions on studies of a narrow segment of the adult population in a specific context—college students in laboratory settings performing complex paper-and-pencil tasks. In a 2000 study, for example, psychologists Patricia Cheng of the University of California, Los Angeles, and Yunnwen Lien of the National Taiwan University in Taipei presented college students with a set of instances that described the blooming frequencies of plants that had been fed plant food of different shapes and colors. After examining each case, students rated on a numerical scale the likelihood or degree of causal influence of each of the factors and/or made predictions regarding outcomes for novel instances—and showed good reliability in doing so. Although such studies highlight the skills that college students display in such tasks, do they represent the cognitive performance of average people in their thinking about everyday affairs?

To address this question, my student Joanna Saab and I went last year to New York City's Pennsylvania Station. We asked 40 people seated in the waiting room if they would spend 10 minutes answering a survey in exchange for five dollars. Virtually all accepted. We explained that a group was trying different combinations of entertainment features at fund-raisers, to see which would sell the most tickets, and showed each person a diagram with some of the results. The sign for the first party listed door prizes, comedian, costumes; its sales were "medium." The second party listed door prizes, auction, costumes; its sales were "high." The third party listed door prizes, auction, comedian, costumes; its sales were "high."

We left the diagram in view as we talked to each of our interviewees, and we asked, "Based on their results, does the auction help ticket sales?" We also asked how certain they were about their answers. They could choose "very certain," "certain," "think so but not certain" or "just guessing." We asked the same questions for each of the three remaining features: comedian, door prizes, costumes.

As you can deduce for yourself [see box on opposite page], if you examine the first and third parties, adding the auction boosts sales. By comparing the second and third parties, you can see that adding a comedian has no effect on sales. Yet the information available is insufficient for assessing the causal status of door prizes or costumes (because they are always present).

Did this diverse group of adults at Penn Station show as much skill in isolating cause and effect as researchers have attributed to college students? Or even the same degree of skill as the four-year-olds described earlier? In a word, no. Overall, they claimed more causal relationships to be present than the evidence justified. Eighty-three percent judged that two or more of the features caused sales to increase, and 45 percent claimed that three or all four of the features did so (remember, the available evidence supported a relation between only one feature—auction—and outcome). Even more striking, most respondents were quite confident that they were correct. For two of the four features, the average certitude reported was greater than "certain" (and tending toward "very certain"), whereas for the other two the average was slightly below "certain." Gender was not a factor: men and women did not differ significantly in either their judgments or levels of certainty.

What made these respondents so sure about which features affected outcome and which did not? We emphasized to them that they should base their conclusions on the results shown for the particular group of people indicated (rather than on their own prior beliefs about the effectiveness of these features); in response to a follow-up query at the end, all respondents indicated that they had done so. Yet their responses revealed that their judgments were in fact influenced by their own ideas about how effective these features ought to be. Respondents judged door prizes to affect outcome (83 percent did so) much more commonly than they judged costumes to affect outcome (33 percent did so), although the evidence with respect to the two features was identical.

To gain further insight, we presented respondents with an additional task [see box on opposite page].

In this second case, there were no correct answers. One cannot make justifiable predictions

Do studies represent the cognitive performance of average people in their thinking about everyday affairs?

given the indeterminate causal status of two of the features: door prizes and costumes. Nevertheless, respondents' certainty regarding the predictions they made remained as high as it had been for their causal judgments. Their predictions, moreover, were informative. For example, to infer whether a respondent judged the auction feature as causal, we compared the predictions the person made for a particular pair of cases—specifically, those two cases that involved door prizes. If the auction was being regarded as causal, predictions for these two cases (one with the auction present and the other with it absent) should have differed. If the auction was being regarded as noncausal, its presence or absence should have had no influence and predictions for these two cases should have been identical. Similarly, comparing the predictions for the two cases involving costumes allowed us to infer whether the respondent judged the comedian as causal.

The implicit judgments that respondents made in the prediction task tended to be inconsistent with the causal judgments they had made in the judgment task when they were asked to indicate explicitly whether a factor was causal ("helped ticket sales"). Only 15 percent made consistent judgments across both tasks. Similarly, people were inconsistent in the implicit causal attributions they made in response to the questions about which features had influenced each of their predictions. Among the 63 percent who had correctly judged the inclusion of a comedian as having no causal effect in the judgment task, for example, a majority nonetheless indicated that the presence or absence of a comedian had influenced their predictions. Particularly difficult was recognizing that a feature whose presence positively affected an outcome would negatively affect the outcome when it was removed.

Reconciling the Inconsistencies

How can we reconcile the inconsistent and incautious causal judgments made by people waiting in a train station—judgments they claimed to be certain of—with the reasoning skills observed in college students and even four-year-olds? The answer is invariably multifaceted. Our respondents took the task seriously and were motivated to answer the questions to the best of their ability to justify receiving their five dollars. But they were unlikely to focus on the task as a reasoning test, designed to assess their mental processes, as readily as would college students, who have become familiar with such tests. The purpose, which most college students recognize, is not to achieve a solution (whether it be maximizing ticket sales or designing a bridge sufficient to support a given weight) but rather to display how they go about tackling the problem. College students have learned to behave accordingly, looking at the information given and determining how they should use it to produce an answer. Unsurprisingly, then, we found that respondents with a college background made sounder judgments than those without it did.

Those who do not possess this "academic" mind-set, in contrast, tend to focus on getting the problem solved and allocate little attention to the mental operations they use in the process. In getting to a solution, they bring to bear everything they know that might be of use. Based on their own prior knowledge that door prizes seem more likely to be a winner for fund-raising than costumes, they judge door prizes as causal—even though the presented evidence provides no support for this difference. Keeping track of how they responded in an earlier part of the interview, so as to maintain consistency, will not help solve the problem and thus is not a high priority. For such people, the best reading of how things look at the moment is what is important. Once a decision is reached, moreover, expressing confidence and certainty is better than wavering.

So who is using the "smarter" approach? Why put old beliefs on hold when evaluating new information? Aren't people most likely to come to the best conclusions if they make use of all they know while reaching them? In many contexts, the answer is yes. Yet being able to evaluate "the information given" to determine exactly what it does (and does not) imply is also an important skill—and not just within the rarefied halls of academia.

Suppose, for example, I am thinking about trying the new weight-loss product my friends are talking about, but they tell me they have

Aren't people most likely to come to the best conclusions if they make use of all they know?

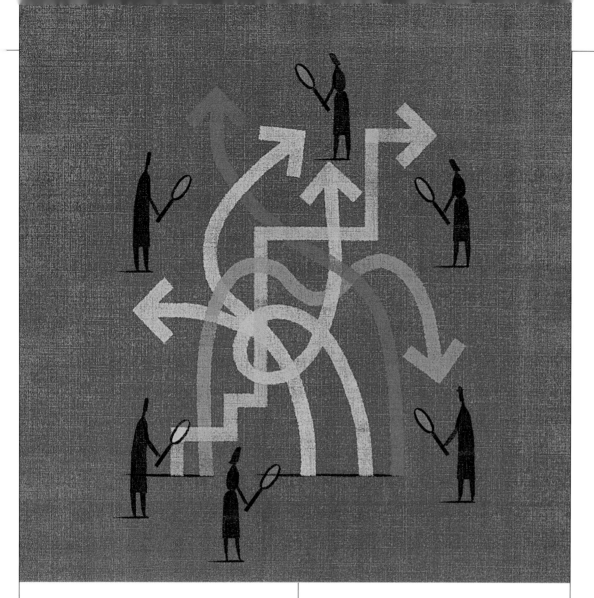

heard it could cause cancer. When I go to the medical library to look up a recent study on the product, I want to be able to interpret what it says, independent of prior thoughts I may have. In reaching a decision, I may ultimately integrate what the report says with other considerations. But I could not do so were I not able to interpret the document in its own right.

In his 2004 book, *The Robot's Rebellion*, Keith E. Stanovich of the University of Toronto similarly makes the case for the importance of what he calls "decontextualized" reasoning and describes studies in which participants fail to use it. The relevance of such reasoning is by no means limited to thinking about causality. Reaching a verdict in a legal trial, for example, is one common context in which jurors are required to rely on the presented evidence alone, not on everything that comes to mind related to this evidence. So is deductive reasoning, employing ancient Greek philosopher Aristotle's classical syllogisms. Stanovich notes, for example, that 70 percent of adult subjects accepted this syllogism as valid:

> **Premise 1:** All living things need water.
> **Premise 2:** Roses need water.
> **Conclusion:** Roses are living things.

Because we know the conclusion to be true in the real world, it is easy to accept, even though it

(The Author)

DEANNA KUHN is professor of psychology and education at Teachers College, Columbia University. She holds a Ph.D. in developmental psychology from the University of California, Berkeley, and was previously at the Graduate School of Education at Harvard University. She is editor of the journal *Cognitive Development* and co-editor of the *Cognition, Perception, and Language* volume of the *Handbook of Child Psychology,* sixth edition (Wiley, 2006). Kuhn is co-author of *The Development of Scientific Thinking Skills* (Academic Press, 1988). Her most recent book, *Education for Thinking* (Harvard University Press, 2005), seeks to identify and examine the thinking skills that we can justify as objectives of education.

does not follow logically from the premises. To be convinced of this fact, we need only compare it with a syllogism identical in form:

> **Premise 1:** All animals of the hudon class are ferocious.
> **Premise 2:** Wampets are ferocious.
> **Conclusion:** Wampets are animals of the hudon class.

Typically only 20 percent of people accept this conclusion as correct. The other 80 percent correctly reject it, the improvement in performance presumably arising because no obfuscating real-world knowledge got in the way.

As the research we conducted at the train sta-tion suggests, decontextualization is not the only skill in the careful reasoner's mental tool kit. Consistency and avoiding undue certainty in one's judgments are also important. Undue cer-tainty reflects a failure in "knowing what you know" (also called metacognition) and underlies the rigidity in thinking that is a major contributor to human strife. Inconsistency can be similarly self-serving, allowing us to protect our favorite theories without subjecting them to the same standards of evidence to which we subject those of others. We maintain that superior skill was the cause of our team's victory, whereas the other team's win was because of luck.

The authors made no assessment of consistency or certainty of the causal judgments of the four-year-olds in the study described earlier. But we can see why these children may have had an easier time evaluating evidence than the adults in our study had. The scenario involving different colored flowers engaged very little in the way of prior knowledge regarding which colors would be more likely to make a monkey sneeze. The adults, in contrast, had much prior experience that they could bring to bear on matters of event planning, ticket sales and the enjoyableness of different activities. This

nable to improvement, and with practice it becomes more careful and critical. Performance on standardized tests of "basic skills" of literacy and numeracy has come to occupy center stage as a measure of how successful schooling has been at teaching students what they need to know. In contrast, learning to make sound judgments about matters of the kind people encounter in everyday life has not been a high priority as an objective of education.

(Rich knowledge can make it more challenging to evaluate evidence in its own right.)

rich knowledge made it more challenging for them to evaluate the evidence in its own right.

What the competence displayed by the subjects in Schulz and Gopnik's study does show, however, is that the underlying reasoning processes entailed in multivariable causal inference (involving multiple potential causes) have developed to at least a rudimentary degree among four-year-olds. More important, this is competence that we can build on in devising the kinds of educational experiences that will help older children and adolescents, and even adults, become more careful causal reasoners.

Other research that my colleagues and I have done shows that both children and adults do come to reason more critically about causality if they are provided frequent opportunities to practice evaluating evidence and making causal judgments and predictions. Early adolescent students initially show the kinds of faulty multivariable causal reasoning that have been illustrated here. But if they engage with problems of this kind over the course of several months, their reasoning improves sharply. The same is true of young adults enrolled in a community college.

Thinking Forward

The message we might glean from the research I have described is twofold. First, the causal reasoning of average adults regarding everyday matters is in fact highly fallible. People frequently make unwarranted inferences with unwarranted certainty, and it is likely that they act on many of these inferences.

Second, although people may leap to unwarranted conclusions in their judgments about causality, we should not jump to the conclusion that this is the way things must be. Thinking is ame-

Such aspects of cognition may be recognized as warranting more attention, as people today struggle to interpret escalating amounts of information about increasingly complex matters, some of which have implications for their very survival. By promoting the development of skills that will help them meet this challenge, we could enrich conceptions of what is important for students to learn. As noted earlier, frequent opportunity to investigate diverse forms of evidence and draw conclusions from them does strengthen reasoning skills. Even getting into the habit of asking oneself and others simple questions like "How do we know?" and "Can we be certain?" goes a long way toward the objective of sound, rigorous thinking.

In an era of escalating pressure on educators to produce the standardized test performance demanded by No Child Left Behind legislation, is it sensible for them to even think about undertaking anything more? Certainly young people must become literate and numerate. But in the end, what could be a more important purpose of education than to help students learn to exercise their minds to make the kinds of careful, thoughtful judgments that will serve them well over a lifetime? M

(Further Reading)

◆ **Who Is Rational? Studies of Individual Differences in Reasoning.** Keith E. Stanovich. Lawrence Erlbaum Associates, 1999.
◆ **The Everyday Production of Knowledge: Individual Differences in Epistemological Understanding and Juror Reasoning Skill.** M. Weinstock and M. A. Cronin in *Applied Cognitive Psychology*, Vol. 17, No. 2, pages 161–181; 2003.
◆ **The Robot's Rebellion: Finding Meaning in the Age of Darwin.** Keith E. Stanovich. University of Chicago Press, 2004.
◆ **Education for Thinking.** Deanna Kuhn. Harvard University Press, 2005.

Freeing a (Locked-In) Mind

Vegetative patients may soon be able to communicate with the outside world

By Karen Schrock

T he patient opens her eyes, but they are unfocused. She is awake yet apparently unaware of anything going on in the hospital room around her. After the accident, she lies in her bed, unresponsive, day after day. What is she thinking?

ANGELA WYANT Getty Images

Soon we may be able to communicate with such "locked-in" minds—trapped in bodies that no longer respond to their mental control. In a blitz of publicity in fall 2006, a team of British researchers announced they had imaged the brain of one of their "vegetative" patients and discovered that she was in fact conscious and aware. Now that same team has developed a way to ask yes-or-no questions of such patients. The idea is radical: we might soon be able to reach a number of people, including 250,000 Americans, who suffer would recover unexpectedly. When someone woke up out of a decade-long coma, the revival would be considered a miracle or, at the very least, a medical mystery. There seemed to be no way to determine if a patient with brain damage would come to or not. The only thing to do was wait and see.

But beginning in the 1970s, the scientific field of neurorehabilitation came into existence. Rehab centers, where patients could receive treatment from specialists, sprang up around the country. Doctors began to consider each brain

Patients can literally communicate without having to say or do anything.

from consciousness disorders—patients who, until now, had been considered beyond treatment.

"We are now able to detect when somebody is consciously aware, when existing clinical methods have been unable to provide that information," says Adrian Owen of the University of Cambridge, leader of the team of researchers who imaged the woman's brain as she responded to doctors' requests that she imagine such activities as playing tennis. Because of recent advances in imaging technology, patients "can literally communicate without having to say or do anything," Owen says.

A Shift in Thinking

"People have felt until now that this patient group isn't worth investing in. The attitude has been, 'There's nothing that can be done,'" Owen adds. Decades ago the medical community provided nothing more than palliative care for patients with disorders of consciousness who could not wake up or who were not aware of their surroundings. These brain-damaged patients were kept clean and comfortable until they died.

Once in a while, however, one of these patients injury individually, tailoring unique drug regimens and physical therapies in an attempt to improve each patient's condition. That was the best they could do, however: traditional magnetic resonance imaging (MRI)—used since the 1980s to map the structure of the brain or other areas inside the body—made it possible for doctors to see physical damage to the brain but did not allow them to examine its activity.

Then, in the 1990s, with the advent of functional MRI (fMRI) scans, it became possible to study activity in living brains. Functional MRI allows researchers to see which areas of the brain are most active during thought processes, which is how Owen and his colleagues determined that their vegetative patient was indeed aware and responding to their commands. Slowly, neuroscientists' understanding of brain damage began to move forward. Brain-damaged patients were no longer automatically considered lost causes but rather victims of a condition for which there might someday be a cure.

"Functional imaging is really the first imaging technique that has allowed us to look at the inner cognitive workings of patients who have disorders of consciousness," says Joy Hirsch, a neuroscientist at Columbia University. In 1992 scientists discovered they could use an MRI scanner to map changes in blood flow to different areas of the brain, signaling which parts of the brain were working during any given thought process or sensory stimulation. In the subsequent decade, researchers determined the difference in the fMRI patterns of willful thought and passive response to stimuli, a crucial distinction when examining the brain of a patient whose state of consciousness is unknown. Now fMRI technol-

FAST FACTS

Trapped No Longer

1 >> Some brain-damaged patients may be conscious of their surroundings but unable to control their body to communicate that awareness.

2 >> Now researchers are using fMRI scanning to "talk" directly to these patients' brains, a breakthrough that could lead to new treatments.

ogy has improved such that researchers can give patients commands and analyze their responses within a minute rather than a month. The result: we are on the verge of communicating with patients who only a few years ago would have been considered brain-dead.

Of course, not all patients can improve: some simply do not have enough brain structure left. "We've seen several recent cases that tell us that in some of these patients there is some chance of recovery," Owen explains. "But certainly not in all patients." This was the case with Terri Schiavo, a permanently vegetative Florida woman who became the center of a political debate in 2005 when her parents challenged her husband's decision to remove her feeding tube and let her die. A computed tomographic (CT) scan showed that much of her brain had atrophied, and doctors were unanimous in their opinion that she would not recover.

Determining a brain-damaged patient's prognosis is not always so cut and dried. The brain is a fragile organ; it can be damaged in many different ways, most of which are poorly understood by science. Whereas a number of patients might regain partial or complete use of their faculties, others truly are permanently injured with no hope of recovery. In a few cases, the victims might be aware of their surroundings but unable to respond. Still others are unconscious *and* unaware. The difficulty lies in determining which patients are which.

The first step is getting a general understanding of the patient's state of mind. Clinicians divide disorders of consciousness into three categories: coma, in which a patient is neither awake nor responsive; vegetative, in which a patient is awake but unresponsive; and minimally conscious, in which a patient is awake and responds to stimuli but has limited capacity to take willful actions. Typically doctors make these categorizations by observing a patient at the bedside. By

this method alone, a patient thought to be vegetative could actually be aware.

"It's really a conundrum. The way that consciousness is typically measured is by basically asking somebody to tell you that they are conscious," Owen says. "So if someone wasn't unconscious but couldn't respond and tell you that, they would be classed as unconscious."

In Owen's team's case study, reported in the September 8, 2006, issue of the journal *Science*, the researchers asked the vegetative patient to

Magnetic resonance imaging (MRI) is now allowing scientists to read the minds of some brain-damaged patients.

(The Author)

KAREN SCHROCK is a staff writer and editor for *Scientific American Mind*.

imagine herself doing various tasks, including walking through the rooms of her home, while they scanned her brain using fMRI. The resulting images [*see box on opposite page*] showed that her response matched that of healthy test subjects—she understood the commands and intentionally decided to comply.

But analyzing the massive volume of data generated by an fMRI scan takes time. When fMRI was first developed, it took up to several months to interpret one scan. As recently as early 2006, when Owen's team scanned the patient's brain, data analysis took many days. "That eureka moment didn't come as she was lying in the scanner," Owen states. "Two weeks later we realized she had indeed been playing tennis in her head."

Now, Owen reports, fMRI technology has advanced to the point where researchers can interpret the data from a scan in 30 or 40 seconds. This breakthrough opens up the possibility of "reading" a person's thoughts at a given moment, enabling a locked-in patient to "speak" with only his or her mind.

New Therapies

Owen and his colleagues hope that one day the new fMRI techniques they are developing will assist doctors in determining which patients are aware but trapped in an unresponsive body, thereby providing a more reliable indication of patients' potential for recovery. The researchers report that their patient who played tennis in her

head subsequently improved from her seemingly vegetative state. Owen points out that by scanning her brain with fMRI, doctors were able to tell she was recovering long before she showed any outward physical signs. Early detection of a brain-damaged patient's potential for recuperation could lead to alternative treatments in the form of more aggressive drug or surgical interventions and to the encouragement of social interactions, such as visits from family members.

Owen's team is currently devising a protocol for "talking" to a vegetative patient's mind, by employing the same basic principles as in its initial test of the tennis player. "If the patient imagines playing tennis, it means 'yes.' If they imagine walking through the rooms of their home, it means 'no,'" Owen says. The different thoughts light up, or activate, various regions in the brain. With some practice on healthy subjects, the researchers have learned to tell apart thought-only responses of "yes" and "no" in under a minute. The doctors are now preparing to test their technique on a vegetative patient whom they have already found to be aware. If they succeed, they will "converse" with a locked-in person for the first time ever.

As with any new technology, it will take several years to understand how best to use fMRI in a clinical setting, and for now, researchers continue to deny most requests to scan brain-damaged patients. "It's not ethical, because we have not completed the research we would need to complete to be absolutely certain that our inter-

Glossary of Consciousness

Doctors define consciousness as having two important components: wakefulness and awareness. Disorders of consciousness are diagnosed when one or both of these elements are impaired.

DIAGNOSIS	AWAKE	AWARE
Coma	No	No
Vegetative state	Yes	No
Minimally conscious state	Yes	Yes, but responsiveness is severely limited

ELLEN CAREY Getty Images

Evidence of Awareness

Researchers discovered that a vegetative patient was actually conscious by comparing her brain activity with that of healthy controls. When the patient and the healthy subjects were asked to imagine playing tennis and walking through the rooms of their homes, their brains showed similar activation in motor and spatial navigation areas.

Tennis Imagery

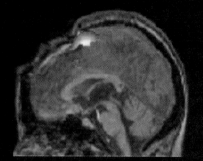

Spatial Navigation Imagery

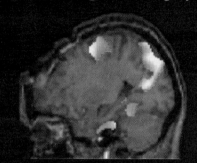

Patient

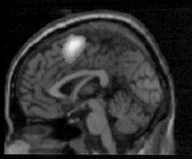

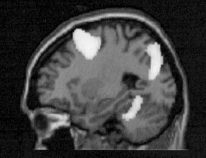

Healthy Volunteers

pretations of the scan are right," says Hirsch,
who fields e-mails from concerned family members on a daily basis. "It's just heart-wrenching, the number of people out there who want to know about the cognitive life of their loved ones who can't respond to them."

For now, using fMRI to diagnose or communicate with brain-damaged patients will continue to happen only in the small number of research laboratories devoted to studying disorders of consciousness. Funding is scarce for investigators studying brain damage, according to both Hirsch and Owen. The equipment is expensive—a state-of-the-art MRI scanner capable of functional scanning costs several million dollars—and scientists have not yet figured out the best way to use the relatively new technology. But with the possibility of being able to communicate with vegetative patients lurking just on the horizon, the researchers hope their work will eventually lead to the widespread release of locked-in minds.

"It's not something that every hospital can start doing yet," Owen says. "But we'd like to develop the technique so we can make it easier and accessible to everyone." **M**

(Further Reading)

◆ **Brain Function in Coma, Vegetative State, and Related Disorders.** Steven Laureys, Adrian M. Owen and Nicholas D. Schiff in *Lancet Neurology,* Vol. 3, No. 9, pages 537–546; September 2004.
◆ **Raising Consciousness.** Joy Hirsch in *Journal of Clinical Investigation,* Vol. 115, No. 5, pages 1102–1103; May 2005.
◆ **The Boundaries of Consciousness: Neurobiology and Neuropathology.** Edited by Steven Laureys. Elsevier Sciences, 2006.
◆ **Detecting Awareness in the Vegetative State.** Adrian M. Owen, Martin R. Coleman, Melanie Boly, Matthew H. Davis, Steven Laureys and John D. Pickard in *Science,* Vol. 313, page 1402; September 8, 2006.

FROM ADRIAN M. OWEN ET AL. IN SCIENCE, VOL. 313, SEPTEMBER 8, 2006. REPRINTED WITH PERMISSION FROM AAAS

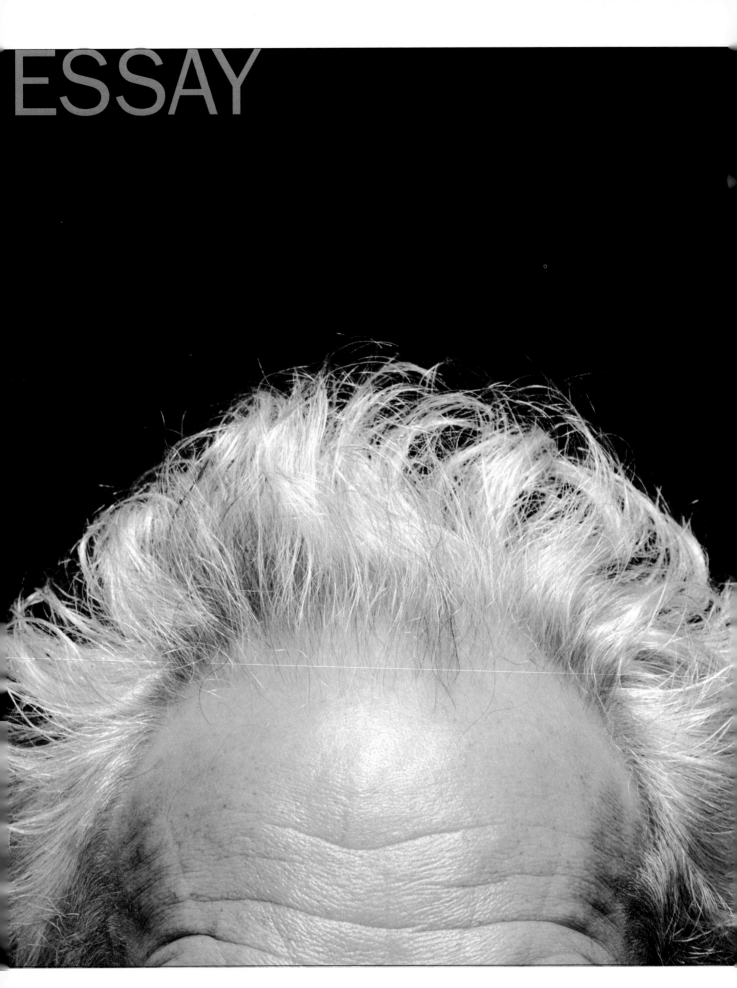

SMARTER on DRUGS

We recoil at the idea of people taking drugs to enhance their intelligence. But why?   By Michael S. Gazzaniga

Any child can tell you that some people are smarter than others. But what is the difference between the brain of a Ph.D. student and the brain of the average Joe? If we can figure that out, then a bigger question follows: Is it ethical to turn average Joes into geniuses? Evolutionary theory suggests that if we are smart enough to invent technology that can increase our brain capacity, we should be able to use that advantage. It is the next step in the survival of the fittest. As noted psychologist Corneliu Giurgea stated in the 1970s, "Man is not going to wait passively for millions of years before evolution offers him a better brain."

That said, gnawing concerns persist when it comes to artificially enhancing intelligence. Geneticists and neuroscientists have made great strides in understanding which genes, brain structures and neurochemicals might be altered artificially to increase intelligence. The fear this prospect brings is that a nation of achievers will discard hard work and turn to prescriptions to get ahead.

Enhancing intelligence is not science fiction. Many "smart" drugs are in clinical trials and could be on the market in less than five years. Some medications currently available to patients with memory disorders may also increase intelligence in the healthy population. Likewise, few people would lament the use of such aids to ameliorate the forgetfulness that aging brings. Drugs that counter these deficits would be adopted gratefully by millions of people.

Drugs designed for psychotherapy can also be used to enhance certain regular mental functions. Just as Ritalin can improve the academic performance of hyperactive children, it can do the same for normal children. It is commonly thought to boost SAT scores by more than 100 points, for both the hyperactive and the normal user. Many healthy young people now use it that way for that purpose, and quite frankly, there is no stopping this abuse.

In a way, with these new compounds, we are reliving the stories associated with better-known illegal psychoactive drugs. Morphine is a terrific help with pain produced by burns and other somatic ills; it is also a mind-altering substance that in some areas of society causes tremendous social and psychological problems. Do we stop developing such painkillers just because they might be misused? Even when the issue is simple memory enhancement, we profess great social concern. Why do we resist changes in our cognitive skills through drugs?

The reason, it seems to me, is that we think cognitive enhancement is cheating. If, somehow, someone gets ahead through hard work, that's okay. But popping a pill and mastering information after having read it only once seems unfair.

This position makes no sense. Among the normal population are men and women with incredible memories, fast learners of language and music, and those with enhanced capabilities of all kinds. Something in their brains allows them to encode new information at lightning speed. We accept the fact that they must have some chemical system that is superior to ours or some neural circuitry that is more efficient. So why should we be upset if the same thing can be achieved with a pill? In some way, we were cheated by Mother Nature if we didn't get the superior neural system, so for us to cheat her back through our own inventiveness seems like a smart thing to do. In my opinion, it is exactly what we should do.

Memory Enhancers

Already available, or making their way through the Federal Drug Administration's approval process, are several cognitive enhancers that reportedly improve memory. These are also being called smart drugs, or nootropes, from the Greek *noos*, for "mind," and *tropein*, for "to-

ward." Whenever a study shows that a certain chemical produces even a moderate increase in memory in an animal population (be it fruit flies, mice or humans), one of two things happens. If the compound is not on the market, a pharmaceutical company quickly jumps in to exploit the finding. If the drug is already on the market but is used to treat a known ailment—for instance, Alzheimer's or attention-deficit hyperactivity disorder—a surge takes place in off-label use, for a purpose other than the intended application. Some regulated smart drugs are currently on the market, as are unregulated herbal medications. Entire stores called smart bars have popped up along the West Coast to sell these items.

Work on memory enhancers may be furthest along. Eric R. Kandel of Columbia University, who won a Nobel Prize for his research on learning and memory in the sea slug *Aplysia,* is one proponent. He found that learning occurs at the synapse (the junction between two neurons) by several means. The synapse is enhanced when a protein called CREB is activated, and CREB plays a role in memory formation in fruit flies and in mice. With these discoveries came the 1998 birth of Memory Pharmaceuticals, Kandel's Montvale, N.J.–based company, which hopes to formulate a drug that will raise the amount of CREB in the human neural system and thus facilitate the formation of long-term memories. One of the most promising chemicals is called MEM 1414. If clinical trials go well, MEM 1414 could be on the market after 2008. At least one other company, Helicon Therapeutics in Farmingdale, N.Y., is also investigating CREB to improve human memory formation.

Alternative drugs are also in the works based on other brain mechanisms. Before a neuron naturally increases CREB, certain channels on its membrane must open to allow positive ions to flow into the cell. The ions then trigger a cascade of events leading to the activation of CREB. One channel of interest is known as NMDA. In 1999 Joseph Z. Tsein, Ya-Ping Tang and their colleagues, then at Princeton University, discovered that increasing the number of NMDA receptors

If we are smart enough to invent technology that increases brain capacity, we should use that advantage.

in the mouse hippocampus led to better performance on a spatial-memory task. Now researchers and pharmaceutical companies are pursuing NMDA receptor agonists (they combine with the receptors) as nootropes. At least a dozen new drugs of this kind are making their way toward clinical trials.

Scientists have known for years that more commonplace chemicals such as adrenaline, glucose and caffeine increase memory and performance. We all know it, too: procrastinators find clarity of mind in the adrenaline rush to meet a deadline; we try not to work "on an empty stomach"; and we are willing to pay a premium for a vente latte—all testimony to our appreciation of these legal activities.

Self-medicating with Starbucks is one thing. But consider the following. In July 2002 Jerome Yesavage and his colleagues at Stanford University discovered that donepezil, a drug approved by the FDA to slow the memory loss of Alzheimer's patients, improves the memory of the normal population. The researchers trained pilots in a flight simulator to perform specific maneuvers and to respond to emergencies that developed during their mock flight, after giving half the pilots donepezil and half a placebo. One month later they retested the pilots and found that those who had taken the donepezil remembered their training better, as shown by improved performance. The possibility exists that donepezil could become a Ritalin for college students. I believe nothing can stop this trend, either.

This anecdote reminds us that the unintended use and misuse of drugs is a constant. Trying to manage it, control it and legislate it will bring nothing but failure and duplicity. This fact of life needs to be aired, and our culture needs to reach a consensus about it. Aricept (the commercial name for donepezil) works, caffeine works, Rit-

alin works. Individuals will use such drugs or not use them, depending on their personal philosophy about enhancement. Some people like to alter their mental states; others do not.

My guess is that, on average, adults will choose not to use memory enhancers or the theoretically more obscure IQ or cognitive enhancers. Why? Because when memory is in the normal range, we adapt to its level and set our personal psychological life in that context. Increasing our memory capacity might send a ripple effect across the landscape of our daily lives. After all, we spend a good part of each evening trying to forget many of the day's memories. Over a lifetime we have built up our personal narrative based on the efficiency of our memory and our capacity to forget. Any significant or even slight change in these capacities will have to be integrated into the backbone of that narrative, changing the mental life of a person.

For a society that spends significant time and money trying to be liberated from past experiences and memories, the arrival of new memory enhancers has a certain irony. Why do people drink, smoke marijuana and engage in other activities that cause them to take leave of their senses? Why are psychiatry offices full of patients with unhappy memories they would like to lose? And why do victims of horrendous emotional events such as trauma, abuse or stressful relationships suffer from their vivid recollections? A pill that enhances memory may lead to a whole new set of disorders. Maybe the haunting memories

(The Author)

MICHAEL S. GAZZANIGA is director of the Center for Cognitive Neuroscience at Dartmouth College and has served on the President's Council on Bioethics. This article is adapted with permission from his new book, *The Ethical Brain* (Dana Press, April 2005). Copyright © 2005 by Dana Press.

of a bad experience will become ever present in consciousness after taking an enhancing pill. This problem and dozens of others may well be the outcome.

Of course, many steps precede success in drug development, and some critics doubt we will see these newer memory enhancers in our lifetime. Although studies on animal models find that certain drugs improve memory or performance on specific tasks, it is not clear that they would help humans. Many nootropes that were promising in lab animals have failed miserably in human clinical trials. Is this because millions of years of evolution have led to a human brain whose neurochemical concentrations are at optimal levels? Another hurdle for drugs is their potential to cause deleterious effects. Some accounts of mice with altered "smart" brains, for instance, show that the mice are not only more receptive to learning but are also more sensitive to pain.

Superintelligence

Enhancing memory is one issue. Making people smarter—more able to contemplate complex ideas with greater ease and facility—somehow seems more problematic. Do we want a nation full of Harvard graduates? On the surface it seems insane. But the basic science suggests that superintelligence is not far-fetched.

Defining what it means to be "smart" has frustrated psychologists for years. IQ and SAT tests, though long-standing indicators of academic success, are far from perfect indicators of success in the "real world." Intelligence tests, especially the IQ test, measure people's analytical skills, verbal comprehension, perceptual organization, working memory and processing speed. This type of intelligence is called psychometric intelligence, and although it is not the only type (some researchers believe in "multiple intelligences," even including athletic ability), it is *testable* and so remains one of our primary gauges.

In 1904 Charles Spearman, an English psychologist, reviewed the literature of the 19th century on intelligence and found that people who performed well on one test of intelligence seemed to perform well on all others. Spearman theorized the existence of a "general intelligence," which he termed g, that is used to process many domains and thus makes some people good at nearly all intelligence challenges. Many investigations since 1904 have supported Spearman's idea, and the current consensus among scientists and psychologists is that a g factor accounts for a great deal of the variance in intelligence test scores.

Recently geneticists have discovered that even such abstract qualities as personality and intelligence are coded for in our genetic blueprint. Studies of the genetic basis of g are just beginning, and because g most likely arises from the influence of many genes, the hunt will be a long one. Yet one study has already found that a gene on chromosome 6 is linked to intelligence.

So-called genetic brain mapping could help the search. Scientists are looking at the structural features (size, volume, and so on) of the brains of many individuals, including twins, familial relatives and unrelated individuals. By scanning all these brains in magnetic resonance imaging machines and looking at the differences, researchers have been able to determine which areas of the brain are most under the control of genes. These studies have emerged only in the past three to four years. Geneticists hope that once they know which brain areas are most affected by heredity, they can figure out which genes are responsible for those regions. With this kind of reverse mapping, the experts should be able to learn more about the genetics of intelligence.

Geneticists and neuroscientists seem to be in agreement: the genes that affect intelligence may be coding for the structure and functions of specific brain areas that underlie Spearman's g. When researchers combine brain mapping with IQ tests, they can begin to tease out the correlations between the size, structure, and volume of brains and intelligence. Neuroscientists have determined that overall brain size has a statistically significant correlation with IQ. More detailed investigations show that the amount of gray matter—consisting mainly of the cell bodies of neurons—in the frontal lobes varies significantly with differ-

DAVIES & STARR Getty Images

A nation of Harvard graduates may seem insane, but basic science suggests it's not far-fetched.

ences in intelligence scores. That suggests the frontal lobe may be the location of g.

Indeed, John Duncan and his colleagues at the Medical Research Council in Cambridge, England, who put smart volunteers through a multitude of mentally demanding tasks, found that the lateral part of the frontal lobe on both the left and right sides may be the resting place of general intelligence. While undergoing positron-emission tomography (PET) scans, Duncan's subjects selectively activated the lateral frontal cortex during several intelligence tests. Some researchers are skeptical of the importance of Duncan's study, saying it is "suggestive" at best because we do not yet fully understand what the frontal lobes do. But his findings solidify the fact that we have entered a new age in scientific history—an era that allows neuroscientists to investigate individual differences in intelligence, previously a field only for psychology.

Accordingly, a robust literature concerning neural differences in intelligence has arisen. Further support for the frontal lobe's role comes from the observation that people with frontal lobe damage usually score 20 to 60 points lower on IQ tests than others. These people also have deficits in what is called fluid intelligence, which decreases with age and includes abstract reasoning, processing speed, accurate responses during time constraints and use of novel materials.

Smarter or Just Faster?

The future is here. We have isolated one gene involved in intelligence, and others will follow. We know which parts of the brain are influenced by particular genes and which parts correlate with high IQ. We also know some of the neurochemicals involved in learning and memory. With such knowledge, we will gain understanding of what needs to be manipulated to increase intelligence in people who were not blessed with brilliance in their genomes or further increase the intelligence of those who were. Gene therapy could insert, delete, turn on or turn off genes that we find to be associated with intelligence.

My own belief is that none of this threatens our sense of self. The opportunities to enhance one's mental state abound. "Smart" describes how well one processes information and figures out tasks. Once something has been figured out, much work must then be applied to the solution, and the smartest people in the world rarely say that the task is easy. They have worked hard to achieve insight and solutions. So we may all get faster at figuring out new problems, but it is not clear what it would mean to get smarter. "Smarter" is frequently just another word for "faster."

Whatever happens, we can be sure that cognitive enhancement drugs will be developed and that they will be used and misused. But just as most people do not choose to alter their mood with Prozac and just as we all reorient our lives in the face of unending opportunities to change our sense of normal, our society will absorb new memory drugs according to each individual's underlying philosophy and sense of self. Self-regulation will occur. The few people who desire altered states will find the means, and those who do not want to alter their sense of who they are will ignore the drug potions. The government should stay out of it, letting our own ethical and moral sense guide us through the new enhancement landscape. M

(Further Reading)

◆ **Intelligence Reframed: Multiple Intelligences for the 21st Century.** Howard Gardner. Basic Books, 2000.
◆ **"Smart Drugs": Do They Work? Are They Ethical? Will They Be Legal?** Steven P. R. Rose in *Nature Reviews Neuroscience,* Vol. 3, No. 12, pages 975–979; December 2002.

Why Do We Cry?

Other animals howl when they are in distress, but only humans weep tears of sorrow—or joy

By Chip Walter

CHRISTOPHER ZACHAROW Getty Images

Nature is loaded with odd traits and behaviors. There are elephant trunks, the widely separated eyes of hammerhead sharks, and the wacky, effervescent mating dances that sandhill cranes do. But nothing is quite as strange as human crying.

The youngest infants cry without tears, to communicate needs or distress.

(Women cry five times a month or so
and men about once every four weeks.)

It does not seem odd to us, of course. We do it often enough ourselves and witness someone else doing it nearly every day. According to one study of more than 300 men and women conducted in 1980s at the University of Minnesota, women cry five times a month or so and men about once every four weeks. And the first thing a baby does when it enters the world is bawl to let everyone know it has arrived healthy and whole. It is not the howling itself that makes our crying unusual; it is the tears that go along with it. Other animals may whimper, moan and wail, but none sheds tears of emotion—not even our closest primate cousins. Apes *do* have tear ducts, as

do other animals, but their job extends only to ocular housecleaning, to bathe and heal the eyes. But in our case, at some point long ago, one of our ancestors evolved a neuronal connection between the gland that generates tears and the parts of the brain that feel, sense and express deep emotion.

Like all genetic mutations, the one that led to tears was a mistake. But it was a mistake that worked. If the wayward gene had not enhanced the survival of the creatures that inherited it, natural selection would have long ago kicked it to the curb. The question is: What advantages come with our special brand of teary-eyed crying? Recently researchers have begun to piece together some answers, and along the way they are uncovering some surprising insights into what makes us tick.

The reasons we cry are many. They range from the primitive—a simple signal of pain or distress—to the mysterious, a sophisticated and highly developed form of communication that bonds humans in ways no other creature can experience. Ultimately this type of bond helped our ancestors survive and thrive and in time allowed our species to emerge as the most successful and cognitively complex of all the creatures on the planet.

Hoots and Howls

Complex behaviors often have simple roots. Crying is one of them. Like other animals, we humans yowl to signal distress, and we start in infancy. During their first three or four months, before babies learn to smile or laugh or gesture, they cry often and with ear-piercing effectiveness. Later, as they edge closer to the first year of life, they cry less often, and they work out other ways to express what they want, such as pointing, grunting, or tossing spoons and food around. (Some babies cannot cry emotional tears until they reach three to six months of age or so.)

Infants develop different cries that send specific messages as they grow older—shrieks and screams of pain, or cries of separation, discomfort or hunger. Each serves as a kind of rudimentary vocabulary that precedes a baby's first words. They all trace their origins to the hoots and howls that other animals, including primates, still use as their primary way of communicating. This fact probably explains why electromyographic studies, which record the electrical activity of skeletal muscles, show that the nerves that operate the mentalis muscle (the one that makes our chins quiver when we are on the verge of tears) or put the lump in our throats or depress the corners of our lips (with the depressor anguli oris muscle) when we are upset are nearly impossible to control consciously. Scientists have also found that babies born without structures above the midbrain can cry, an indication that the roots of crying run deep into our evolutionary past to a time long before the apparatuses of speech and conscious thought emerged.

Cocktails for Crying

Our reasons for crying grow more varied as we enter adulthood. The deeper emotions that maturity brings seep into the mix, and the messages communicated by our cries extend beyond simple physical discomfort or the basics of survival. This transition does not mean physiology is no longer at work. It is, and it now has become more deeply tied to higher brain function and our increasingly subtle emotional needs. And the change means that tears themselves play a larger role as a signal to others that the emotions we are feeling are strong and genuine.

Emotional tears are one of three kinds of tears we produce. The other two share a similar

Animals use tears only for "housekeeping"—to bathe or heal eyes.

FLIP NICKLIN *Minden Pictures*

Distressed animals may cry, but without emotional tears.

Frey believes these chemical cocktails are linked to the moods and emotions associated with crying. High concentrations of manganese, for example, occur in the brains of people suffering from chronic depression. Excessive ACTH indicates increased anxiety and stress. And higher levels of prolactin in women's bodies may explain why they cry more often than men do, especially after puberty.

Because so many hormones exist in emotional tears, Frey has speculated that crying is the body's way of flushing out the chemicals that are present when we are experiencing strong feelings. This is why, he says, we sometimes counsel one another, "Go ahead. Have a good cry."

But not all scientists agree. It is difficult to prove that tears alone can flush enough hormones from our bodies to provide the sense of relief we often feel after crying. Our tear ducts simply are not that big or that efficient. Even a good, long, heaving bout of sobbing produces only a thimble full of hormone-laden tears. So is some other mechanism at work that leads to the relief we feel when we cry?

Maybe, and it may not be all that mysterious. You might call it the Goldilocks principle. All natural systems struggle to maintain a state of equilibrium in the face of the forces around them. They work to remain neither too hot nor too cold, neither too active nor too lethargic. If the environment swings them in one direction, they counter by pulling back to the middle, "normal" ground as quickly as possible. Rain forests, guppies and humans all seek out their comfort zones. The very same primal need to maintain a middle ground may help explain why we cry.

The autonomic nervous system controls so-called mindless operations such as breathing and heartbeat as well as the basic functioning of organs such as the kidneys and brain. The autonomic nervous system itself is divided into two subsystems, the sympathetic and the parasympathetic. The role of both in crying is controversial but intriguing. The sympathetic nervous system prepares us for fight or flight—physically, mentally and emotionally. When we are scared, the sympathetic nervous system fires off messages that prepare our body to stand its ground and do battle—or to skedaddle. The parasympathetic nervous system then pulls us back to normalcy afterward.

Since the 1960s researchers have theorized that we cry because we are upset, not because we are seeking relief, and that our sympathetic nervous system must therefore govern weeping. But

chemistry, although they perform different functions. Basal tears bathe our eyes each time we blink. Reflex tears well up when we get poked in the eyes or when the fumes from the onions we are cutting irritate them. But emotional tears have a makeup all their own—one that provides some clues about their function. William H. Frey II, a biochemist at the University of Minnesota, has found that they carry 20 to 25 percent more types of protein and have four times the amount of potassium than reflex tears, as well as 30 times the concentration of manganese than human blood serum. They are also loaded with hormones, such as adrenocorticotropin (ACTH), which humans produce when under stress, and prolactin, which controls the neurotransmitter receptors in the lacrimal glands that release tears.

(The Author)

CHIP WALTER is an internationally published science author who writes about the perplexing behavior of *Homo sapiens* and the technologies they create. His latest book is *Thumbs, Toes and Tears—And Other Traits That Make Us Human* (Walker Books, 2006).

FRANS LANTING *Minden Pictures*

just as many scientists have held the opposite view. They argue that crying is an involuntary way of calming down. There have been plenty of studies, but none has been conclusive because it is difficult to induce and measure genuine grief and crying in a laboratory. Nevertheless, researchers such as James J. Gross of Stanford University have tried and subsequently have speculated that even though crying does seem to upset us, and those around us, it may ultimately have a calming effect. Other studies have shown that if the nerves central to the sympathetic system are paralyzed, patients cry more; when important parasympathetic nerves are damaged, they cry less. Those findings suggest that we do not cry because we are upset but because we are trying to get *over* being upset. In other words, crying resets the breaker on our emotional circuit.

If that is the case, then crying exemplifies the Goldilocks principle, physiologically at least. After all, following every fight or flight, every close call or every tense situation, we have to settle down. If we did not, we would blow an aorta or have a stroke and that would be the end of that. Given the dangers our ancestors coped with, a means for calming down would have been not only useful but also downright necessary; otherwise they might have been wiped out in a series of cerebrovascular accidents or a rash of coronary thromboses.

Jungle Truth

None of these findings precisely explains why we cry tears. Why should crying "hot tears" of emotion, as Shakespeare's Lear put it, make good evolutionary sense? They blur our vision and add to the vulnerability that our scrambled emotions have already created. Our social nature may provide a clue. No primate is more deeply bonded to other primates than humans are to one another. Our kind grew up on the savanna, not in the jungle, and had no shortage of dangers to encourage cooperation for survival. But we also compete with one another. Anyone who has been involved

Springing upward before fleeing enhances survival by sending a message to a predator: "I am too fast for you to catch." Likewise, human tears of emotion send signals that help to bond social groups together for survival.

GETTY IMAGES

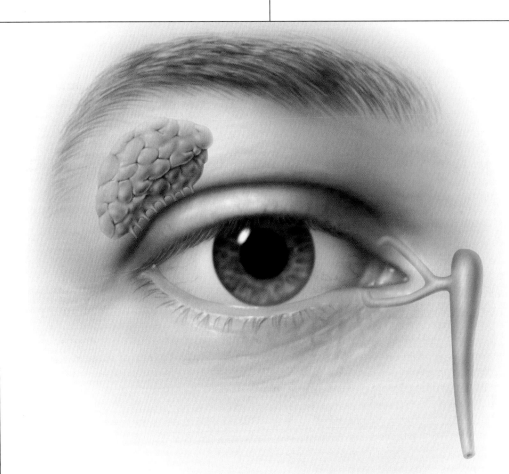

At some point in human evolution, tear ducts somehow became connected to the emotional centers in the brain.

in office politics or high school cliques knows that. Our higher intelligence has only made our coalitions and competitions more complex. So our affairs, as they evolved from early hominid to human, must have favored traits that improve communication, from subtle body language and facial expressions to speech and ... tears.

In 1975 Amotz Zahavi, a biologist at Tel Aviv University, conceived an interesting theory about how animal behaviors and traits that seem detrimental to survival often turn out to be perfectly useful. Why, for example, does a peacock have an enormous and colorful tail when the tail slows the bird down, draws the attention of predators and interferes with flying? Or why does a gazelle, when it senses a lion is about to attack, bound straight up into the air like a pogo stick before making its exit?

These traits and behaviors are examples of what Zahavi called the "handicap principle." On the surface they come at a high price—they require energy and resources and attract dangerous amounts of attention. But, Zahavi speculated, they also send powerful messages. Take the gazelle's first vertical bound, which puts it at an immediate disadvantage: it has lost precious moments that it could have used to distance itself from the predator that intends to make a meal of

it. But such a leap also says, "I am so fast and can jump so high, you will never catch me. So don't waste your energy." Often the lion or cheetah poised for the kill absorbs the message, performs a quick, primal cost-benefit analysis and walks away in search of less vigorous prey.

Tears may serve a similar purpose in a species as intensely social as ours. They are noticeable, and the blurred vision they cause is a hindrance. That makes them costly. Because tears appear only when a person feels very deep emotions, they are not easy to fake. They send an unmistakable, Zahavian signal that the feelings behind them are absolutely real and, therefore, should be taken seriously. Tears, after all, reveal us at our most vulnerable. When we have reached the point where we are crying, the walls are down and our defenses have been breached. The intense emotional bonds forged partly by the binding ties of crying may have helped human communities band together more successfully than they would have otherwise.

Crying Wolf

Mothers tend to respond quickly to the tearless crying of their infants, who are so clearly helpless. But later, in toddlerhood, the situation changes. Crying, like all forms of communication, can be (and is) used to manipulate. Children, even as they grow older, want the attention of their parents. Because crying has been their most effective way of getting it, they continue to do it, even when they do not absolutely need help for basic survival.

Dario Maestripieri, a primatologist at the University of Chicago, has found that infant rhesus macaques share this behavior. They cry out to their mothers in infancy and tend to howl and whimper even more around the time their mothers wean them. At first, macaque mothers come running, but as the cries increase they respond less, because so many of the alarms turn out to be false. Eventually the macaque moms grow more skeptical, and the infants cry less because it does not bring the reassuring attention they seek. As a result, the young monkeys also grow more independent, which in the long run improves their chances of survival.

In the case of people, tears give mothers an extra tool for detecting if a toddler is crying wolf. Every parent has experienced the tearless crying (a.k.a. whining) of a child who is unhappy and wants attention but is not really in trouble. Parents quickly learn to look for real tears if a child cries, a sure sign that their toddler truly needs help.

Soothsaying

Randolph R. Cornelius, a psychology professor at Vassar College and an expert on human crying, has done some of the most interesting research on tears as a kind of instinctual soothsayer. Since 2000 Cornelius and his students have been gathering still photographs and video images from news magazines and television programs recorded all over the world, all of them of people crying real and visible tears. When they find a particularly appropriate image, they prepare two versions: one, the original, with tears, and another with the tears digitally erased.

Cornelius and his colleagues then sit down with volunteers one at a time in front of a computer monitor to watch a slide show. Each slide presents two pictures: one tearful, the other a different picture with the tears secretly erased. No participants are allowed to see the same picture with *and* without tears. The investigators then ask each participant to explain what emotion the person in each photograph is experiencing and how he or she would respond to a person with that particular expression.

The test's observers universally registered that people in pictures with wet eyes or tears rolling down their cheeks were feeling and expressing deeper emotions—mostly sadness—than those who were tearless. But when participants looked at pictures in which the tears had been digitally removed, they were confused about what people were feeling and guessed everything from grief to awe to boredom. Cornelius's conclusion: tears append a crucial communicative dimension to our crying. They add one more true and powerful arrow to the quiver from which we draw our many forms of human communication.

Raw Emotion and High Intelligence

During the past six million years, enormous changes have taken place in our ancestral lineage, much of it from the neck up. Our brains doubled in size and then doubled again. Our faces also have changed, and with them so have our ways of conveying emotion. The rich, expressive musculature evolved by chance but remained with us because it helped us more precisely communicate with, and sometimes manipulate, one another. The parts of the brain associated with the experience and expression of emotion somehow became connected, quite literally, to the lacrimal gland that sits above each of our eyes.

Complex relationships beg for similarly complex forms of communication. For our kind, language was one mighty adaptation that served that purpose. Tears, with the strong, highly visible messages they send, became another. They married raw emotion with a human brain capable of reflecting on those howling, primal feelings. They help us express overwhelming emotions that well up from the primal side of us and linger beyond the reach of words. We all know the feeling, whether it is profound sadness, frustration, joy, pride or pain. Tears take us where syntax and syllables cannot. Without them, we would not be human. **M**

(Further Reading)

◆ **Biological Signals as Handicaps.** A. Grafen in *Journal of Theoretical Biology*, Vol. 144, No. 4, pages 517–546; June 21, 1990.
◆ **The Science of Emotion: Research and Tradition in the Psychology of Emotion.** Randolph R. Cornelius. Prentice-Hall, 1995.
◆ **The Handicap Principle: A Missing Piece of Darwin's Puzzle.** Amotz Zahavi et al. Oxford University Press, 1997.
◆ **The Symbolic Species: The Co-Evolution of Language and the Brain.** Terrence W. Deacon. W. W. Norton, 1998.
◆ **Crying: A Natural and Cultural History of Tears.** Tom Lutz. W. W. Norton, 2001.
◆ **A Darwinian Look at a Wailing Baby.** Carl Zimmer in *New York Times;* March 8, 2005.
◆ **Maternal Effects in Mammals.** Edited by Dario Maestripieri and Jill M. Mateo. University of Chicago Press (in press).

Photographs prove tricky to many toddlers because they have not mastered dual representation: awareness that a symbolic object is itself (in this case, a photograph) as well as a representation of something else (a sneaker). Many try to interact with objects in photographs, such as attempting to put a foot in a shoe.

Mindful of SYMBOLS

On the way to learning that one thing can represent another,
young children often conflate the real item and its symbol.
These errors show how difficult it is to start thinking symbolically
BY JUDY S. DeLOACHE

Photographs by Randy Harris

About 20 years ago I had one of those wonderful moments when research takes an unexpected but fruitful turn. I had been studying toddler memory and was beginning a new experiment with two-and-a-half- and three-year-olds. For the project, I had built a small-scale model of a room that was part of my lab. The real space was furnished like a standard living room, with an upholstered couch, an armchair, a cabinet and so on. The miniature items were as similar as possible: they were the same shape and material, covered with the same fabric and arranged in the same positions. For the study, a child watched as we hid a miniature toy—a plastic dog we dubbed "Little Snoopy"—in the model, which we referred to as "Little Snoopy's room." We then encouraged the child to find "Big Snoopy," a large version of the toy "hiding in the same place in his big room." We wondered whether children could use their memory to figure out where to find the toy in the large room.

The three-year-olds were very successful. After they observed the small toy being placed behind the miniature couch, they ran into the real room and found the large toy behind the real couch. But the two-and-a-half-year-olds, much to my and their parents' surprise, failed abysmally. They cheerfully ran into the big room, but most of them had no idea where to look, even though they remembered where the tiny toy was hidden in the miniature room and could readily find it there.

Their failure to use what they knew about the model to draw an inference about the room indicated that they did not appreciate the relation between the model and room. I soon realized that my memory study was instead a study of symbolic understanding and that the younger children's failure might be telling us something interesting about how and when youngsters acquire the ability to understand that one object can stand for another.

What most distinguishes humans from other creatures is our ability to create and manipulate a wide variety of symbolic representations. This capacity enables us to transmit information from one generation to another, making culture possible, and to learn vast amounts without having direct experience—we all know about dinosaurs despite never having met one. Because of the fundamental role of symbolization in almost everything we do, perhaps no aspect of human development is more important than becoming symbol-minded. What could be more fascinating, I concluded, than finding out how young children begin to use and understand symbolic objects and how they come to master some of the symbolic items ubiquitous in modern life?

Pictures Come to Life

The first type of symbolic object infants and young children master is pictures. No symbols seem simpler to adults, but my colleagues and I have discovered that infants initially find pictures perplexing. The problem stems from the duality inherent in all symbolic objects: they are real in and of themselves and, at the same time, are representations of something else. To understand them, the viewer must achieve dual representation: he or she must mentally represent the object as well as the relation between it and what it stands for.

A few years ago I became intrigued by anecdotes suggesting that infants do not appreciate the dual nature of pictures. I would hear of a baby who tried to pick up a depicted apple or to fit a foot into a photograph of a shoe. My colleagues—David H. Uttal of Northwestern University, Sophia L. Pierroutsakos of St. Louis Community College and Karl S. Rosengren of the University of Illinois—and I decided to investigate even though we assumed such behaviors would be rare and therefore difficult to study. Fortunately, we were wrong.

We began testing infants' understanding of pictures in a very simple way. We put a book containing highly realistic color photographs of individual objects in front of nine-month-olds. To our surprise, every child in the initial study, and most in our subsequent studies, reached out to feel,

that a picture merely represents a real thing. Instead of manipulating the depicted object, they point to it and name it or ask someone else for the name. In 2004 Melissa A. Preissler of Yale University and Susan Carey of Harvard University provided a good example of this development. The two researchers used a simple line drawing of a whisk to teach 18- and 24-month-olds the word for this object that they had not seen before. Most of the children assumed the word referred to the object itself, not just to the picture of it. They interpreted the picture symbolically—as standing for, not just being similar to, its referent.

One factor we think contributes to the decline

> Symbolic representation **enables us to learn** vast amounts about dinosaurs despite never having met one.

rub, pat or scratch the pictures. Sometimes the infants even grasped at the depicted objects as if trying to pick them up off the page.

We had a unique opportunity to see how universal this response was when anthropologist Alma Gottlieb of the University of Illinois took some of our books and a video camera to a remote Beng village in Ivory Coast. Beng babies sat on the ground or in their mother's lap as chickens and goats wandered around and other children and villagers played, worked, talked and laughed nearby. Yet the Beng babies, who had almost certainly never seen a picture before, manually explored the depicted objects just as the American babies had.

The confusion seems to be conceptual, not perceptual. Infants can perfectly well perceive the difference between objects and pictures. Given a choice between the two, infants choose the real thing. But they do not yet fully understand what pictures are and how they differ from the things depicted (the "referents"), and so they explore: some actually lean over and put their lips on the nipple in a photograph of a bottle, for instance. They only do so, however, when the depicted object is highly similar to the object it represents, as in color photographs. The same confusion occurs for video images. Pierroutsakos and her colleague Georgene L. Troseth of Vanderbilt University found that nine-month-olds seated near a television monitor will reach out and grab at objects moving across the screen. But when objects bear less resemblance to the real thing—as in a line drawing—infants rarely explore them.

By 18 months, babies have come to appreciate

of manual exploration of pictures is the development of inhibitory control. Throughout the first years of life, children become increasingly capable of curbing impulses. This general developmental change is supported by changes in the frontal cortex. Increased inhibitory control presumably helps infants restrain their impulse to interact directly with pictures, setting the stage for them to simply look, as adults do.

Experience with pictures must play a role in this development as well. In an image-rich society, most children encounter family photographs and picture books on a daily basis. From such interactions, children learn how pictures differ from objects, and they come to appreciate images as targets of contemplation and conversation, not action.

Nevertheless, it takes several years for the nature of pictures to be completely understood. John H. Flavell of Stanford University and his colleagues have found, for example, that until the age of four, many children think that turning a picture of a bowl of popcorn upside down will result in the depicted popcorn falling out of the bowl.

Pictures are not the only source of symbol confusion for very young children. For many years, my colleagues and students and I watched toddlers come into the lab and try to sit down on the tiny chair from the scale model—much to the astonishment of all present. At home, Uttal and Rosengren had also observed their own daughters trying to lie down in a doll's bed or get into a miniature toy car. Intrigued by these remarkable behaviors that were not mentioned in the scientific literature, we decided to study them.

Scale errors, another example of failed dual representation, are common among 18- to 30-month-olds. They interact with small objects as they would with larger versions. This boy kept falling off the chair. (In experiments, objects can be even smaller.)

Gulliver's Errors

We brought 18- to 30-month-old children into a room that contained, among other things, three large play objects: an indoor slide, a child-size chair and a car toddlers could get inside of and propel around the room with their feet. After a child had played with each of the objects at least twice, he or she was escorted from the room. We then replaced the large items with identical miniature versions, only about five inches tall. When the child returned, we did not comment on the switch and let him or her play spontaneously.

We then examined films of the children's behavior for what we came to call scale errors: earnest attempts to perform actions that are clearly impossible because of extreme differences in the relative size of the child's body and the target object. We were very conservative in what we counted as a scale error.

Almost half the children committed one or more of these mistakes. They attempted with apparent seriousness to perform the same actions. Some sat down on the little chair: they walked up to it, turned around, bent their knees and lowered themselves onto it. Some simply perched on top, others sat down so hard that the chair skittered out from under them. Some children sat on the miniature slide and tried to ride down it, usually falling off in the process; others attempted to climb the steps, causing the slide to tip over. (With the chair and slide made of sturdy plastic and being so small, the toddlers faced no danger of hurting themselves.) A few kids tried to get into the tiny car; they opened the door and attempted—often with remarkable persistence—to force a foot inside.

Interestingly, most of the children showed little or no reaction to their failed attempts. A couple seemed a bit angry, a few looked sheepish, but most simply went on to do something else. We think the lack of reaction probably reflects the fact that toddlers' daily lives are full of unsuccessful attempts to do one thing or another.

Our interpretation of scale errors is that they originate in a dissociation between the use of visual information for planning an action and for controlling its execution. When a child sees a miniature, visual information—the object's shape, color, texture and so on—activates the child's mental representation of its referent. Associated with that memory is the motor program for interacting with the large object and other similar objects. In half the children we studied, this motor program was presumably activated but then inhibited, and the children did not attempt to interact with the miniature in the same way.

But in the other half the motor routine was not inhibited. Once the child began to carry out the typical motor sequence, visual information about the actual size of the object was used to accurately perform the actions. Some children, for instance, bent over the tiny chair and looked between their legs to precisely locate it; those trying to get into the miniature car first opened its door and then tried to shove their foot right in. The

(The Author)

JUDY S. DeLOACHE specializes in early cognitive development—specifically of symbolic thinking—at the University of Virginia, where she is professor of psychology. DeLoache also holds an appointment in psychology at the University of Illinois, where she earned her doctorate and has taught since the late 1970s.

Two-year-olds have difficulty appreciating the symbolic relation between a model of a room and a room itself. This boy can see the toy hidden behind the plant in the model but does not know to look for it behind the real plant.

children relied on visual information linking the replica to the normal-size object, but in executing their plan, they used visual information about the miniature's actual size to guide their actions. This dissociation in the use of visual information is consistent with influential theories of visual processing—ones positing that different regions of the brain handle object recognition and planning versus the execution and control of actions.

The Magical Machine

Scale errors involve a failure of dual representation: children cannot maintain the distinction between a symbol and its referent. We know this because the confusion between referent and symbolic object does not happen when the demand for dual representation is eliminated—a discovery I made in 1997 when Rosengren and Kevin F. Miller of the University of Illinois and I convinced two-and-a-half-year-olds—with the full consent of their parents, of course—that we had a device that could miniaturize everyday objects.

Using our amazing shrinking machine, we hoped to see if the need to think of an object in two ways at once was at the heart of children's symbol difficulties. If a child believes that a machine has shrunk an object or a room, then in the child's mind the miniature is the thing itself. There is no symbolic relation between room and model, so children should be able to apply what they know about the big version to the little one.

We used the powers of our device to shrink toys and a large tent. In front of the child, we placed a toy—a troll doll with vivid purple hair—in a tent and aimed the shrinking machine at the tent. The child and experimenter then decamped to another room to wait while the machine did its work. When they returned to the lab, a small tent sat where the big one had been.

When we asked the children to search for the toy, they immediately looked in the small tent. Believing the miniature to actually be the original tent after shrinking, they successfully retrieved the hidden toy. Unlike in our scale model experiment, they had no dual representation to master: the small tent was the same as the large tent, and thus the toy was where it should be, according to the toddlers' view of the world.

Understanding the role of dual representation in how young children use symbols has important practical applications. One has to do with the practice of using dolls to interview young children in cases of suspected sexual abuse. The victims of abuse are often very young children, who are quite difficult to interview. Consequently, many professionals—including police officers, social workers and mental health professionals—employ anatomically detailed dolls, assuming that a young child will have an easier time describing what happened using a doll. Notice that this assumption entails the further assumption that a young child will be able to think of this object as both a doll and a representation of himself or herself.

These assumptions have been called into question by Maggie Bruck of Johns Hopkins University, Stephen J. Ceci of Cornell University, Peter

A. Ornstein of the University of North Carolina at Chapel Hill and their many colleagues. In several independent studies, these investigators have asked preschool children to report what they remember about a checkup with their pediatrician, which either had or had not included a genital check. Anatomically detailed dolls were sometimes used to question the children, sometimes not. In general, the children's reports were more accurate when they were questioned without a

with symbolic objects on young children's learning about letters and numbers. Using blocks designed to help teach math to young children, we taught six- and seven-year-olds to do subtraction problems that require borrowing. We taught a comparison group to do the same but using pencil and paper. Both groups learned to solve the problems equally well—but the group using the blocks took three times as long to do so. A girl who used the blocks offered us some advice after the study:

Common failures show that **using dolls** to interview young children about sexual abuse may be faulty.

doll, and they were more likely to falsely report genital touching when a doll was used.

Based on my research, I suspected that very young children might not be able to relate their own body to a doll. In a series of studies in my lab using an extremely simple mapping task, Catherine Smith placed a sticker somewhere on a child—on a shoulder or foot, for example—and asked the child to place a smaller version of the sticker in the same place on a doll. Children between three and three-and-a-half usually placed the sticker correctly, but children younger than three were correct less than half the time. The fact that these very young children cannot relate their own body to the doll's in this extremely simple situation with no memory demands and no emotional involvement supports the general case against the use of anatomically detailed dolls in forensic situations with young children. (Because of many demonstrations akin to this one, the use of dolls with children younger than five is viewed less favorably than in the past and has been outlawed in some states.)

Educational Ramifications

The concept of dual representation has implications for educational practices as well. Teachers in preschool and elementary school classrooms around the world use "manipulatives"—blocks, rods and other objects designed to represent numerical quantity. The idea is that these concrete objects help children appreciate abstract mathematical principles. But if children do not understand the relation between the objects and what they represent, the use of manipulatives could be counterproductive, as some research suggests.

Meredith Amaya of Northwestern University, Uttal and I are now testing the effect of experience

"Have you ever thought of teaching kids to do these with paper and pencil? It's a lot easier."

Dual representation also comes into play in popular books for children that include flaps that can be lifted to reveal pictures, levers that can be pulled to animate images, and so forth.

Graduate student Cynthia Chiong and I reasoned that these manipulative features might distract children from information presented in the book. Accordingly, we recently used different types of books to teach letters to 30-month-old children. One was a simple, old-fashioned alphabet book, with each letter clearly printed in simple black type accompanied by an appropriate picture—the traditional "A is for apple, B is for boy." Another book had a variety of manipulative features. The children who had been taught with the plain book subsequently recognized more letters than did those taught with the more complicated book. Presumably, the children could more readily focus their attention with the plain 2-D book.

As these various studies show, infants and young children are confused by many aspects of symbols that seem intuitively obvious to adults. They have to overcome hurdles on the way to achieving a mature conception of what symbols represent, and today many must master an ever expanding variety of symbols. Perhaps a deeper understanding of the various stages of becoming symbol-minded will enable researchers to address learning problems that might stem from difficulty grasping the meanings of symbols. **M**

(Further Reading)
◆ **Becoming Symbol-Minded.** J. S. DeLoache in *Trends in Cognitive Sciences*, Vol. 8, No. 2, pages 66–70; February 2004.
◆ Images of children making symbol-related errors can be seen at **www.faculty.virginia.edu/childstudycenter/home.html**

EXPLODING THE SELF-ESTEEM MYTH

BOOSTING PEOPLE'S SENSE OF SELF-WORTH HAS BECOME A NATIONAL PREOCCUPATION. YET SURPRISINGLY, RESEARCH SHOWS THAT SUCH EFFORTS DO LITTLE TO IMPROVE ACADEMIC PERFORMANCE OR PREVENT TROUBLESOME BEHAVIOR

BY ROY F. BAUMEISTER, JENNIFER D. CAMPBELL, JOACHIM I. KRUEGER AND KATHLEEN D. VOHS

People intuitively recognize the importance of self-esteem to their psychological health, so it isn't particularly remarkable that most of us try to protect and enhance it in ourselves whenever possible. What *is* remarkable is that attention to self-esteem has become a communal concern, at least for Americans, who see a favorable opinion of oneself as the central psychological source from which all manner of positive outcomes spring. The corollary, that low self-esteem lies at the root of individual and thus societal problems, has sustained an ambitious social agenda for decades. Indeed, campaigns to raise people's sense of self-worth abound.

Consider what transpired in California in the late 1980s. Prodded by State Assemblyman John Vasconcellos, Governor George Deukmejian set up a task force on self-esteem and personal and social responsibility. Vasconcellos argued that raising self-esteem in young people would reduce crime, teen pregnancy, drug abuse, school underachievement and pollution, and even help to balance the state budget, a prospect predicated on the observation that people with high self-regard earn more than others and thus pay more in taxes. Along with its other activities, the task force as-

sembled a team of scholars to survey the relevant literature. The results appeared in *The Social Importance of Self-Esteem* (University of California Press, 1989), which stated that "many, if not most, of the major problems plaguing society have roots in the low self-esteem of many of the people who make up society." In reality, the report contained little to support that assertion.

In 1995 Edward F. Diener and Brian Wolsic of the University of Illinois and Frank Fujita of Indiana University South Bend examined this possibility. They obtained self-esteem scores from a broad sample of the population and then photographed everybody, presenting these pictures to a panel of judges, who evaluated the subjects for attractiveness. Ratings based on full-length photographs

Findings even suggest that artificially boosting self-esteem may lower performance.

The California task force disbanded in 1995, but a nonprofit organization called the National Association for Self-Esteem (NASE) has picked up its mantle. Vasconcellos, until recently a California state senator, is on the advisory board.

Was it reasonable for leaders in California to start fashioning therapies and social policies without supportive data? Perhaps, given that they had problems to address. But one can draw on many more studies now than was the case 15 years ago, enough to assess the value of self-esteem in several spheres. Regrettably, those who have been pursuing self-esteem-boosting programs, including the leaders of NASE, have not shown a desire to examine the new work, which is why the four of us recently came together under the aegis of the American Psychological Society to review the scientific literature.

In the Eye of the Beholder

Gauging the value of self-esteem requires, first of all, a sensible way to measure it. Most investigators just ask people what they think of themselves. Naturally enough, the answers are often colored by the common tendency to want to make oneself look good. Unfortunately, psychologists lack good methods to judge self-esteem.

Consider, for instance, research on the relation between self-esteem and physical attractiveness. Several studies have generally found clear positive links when people rate themselves on both properties. It seems plausible that physically attractive people would end up with high self-esteem because they are treated more favorably than unattractive ones—being more popular, more sought after, more valued by lovers and friends, and so forth. But it could just as well be that those who score highly on self-esteem scales by claiming to be wonderful people all around also boast of being physically attractive.

showed no significant correlation with self-esteem. When the judges were shown pictures of just the participants' unadorned faces, the correlation between attractiveness and self-esteem was once again zero. In that same investigation, however, self-reported physical attractiveness was found to have a strong correlation with self-esteem. Clearly, those with high self-esteem are gorgeous in their own eyes but not necessarily to others.

This discrepancy should be sobering. What seemed at first to be a strong link between physical good looks and high self-esteem turned out to be nothing more than a pattern of consistency in how favorably people rate themselves. A parallel phenomenon affects those with low self-esteem, who are prone to floccinaucinihilipilification, a highfalutin word (among the longest in the Oxford English Dictionary) but one that we can't resist using here, it being defined as "the action or habit of estimating as worthless." That is, people with low self-esteem are not merely down on themselves; they are negative about everything.

This tendency has certainly distorted some assessments. For example, psychologists once thought that people with low self-esteem were especially prejudiced. But thoughtful scholars, such as Jennifer Crocker of the University of Michigan at Ann Arbor, questioned this conclusion. After all, if people rate themselves negatively, it is hard to label them as prejudiced for rating people not like themselves similarly. When one uses the difference between the subjects' assessments of their own group and their ratings of other groups as the yardstick for bias, the findings are reversed: people with *high* self-esteem appear to be more prejudiced. Floccinaucinihilipilification also raises the danger that those who describe themselves disparagingly may describe their lives similarly, thus furnishing the appearance that low self-esteem has unpleasant outcomes.

Given the often misleading nature of self-reports, we set up our review to emphasize objective measures wherever possible—a requirement that greatly reduced the number of relevant studies (from more than 15,000 to about 200). We were also mindful to avoid another fallacy: the assumption that a correlation between self-esteem and some desired behavior establishes causality. Indeed, the question of causality goes to the heart of the debate. If high self-esteem brings about certain positive outcomes, it may well be worth the effort and expense of trying to instill this feeling. But if the correlations mean simply that a positive self-image is a result of success or good behavior—which is certainly plausible—there is little to be gained by raising self-esteem alone. We began our two-year effort by reviewing studies relating self-esteem to academic performance.

School Daze

At the outset, we had every reason to hope that boosting self-esteem would be a potent tool for helping students. Logic suggests that having a good dollop of self-esteem would enhance striving and persistence in school, while making a student less likely to succumb to paralyzing feelings of incompetence or self-doubt. Modern studies have, however, cast doubt on the idea that higher self-esteem actually induces students to do better.

Such inferences about causality are possible when the subjects are examined at two different times, as was the case in 1986 when Sheila M. Pottebaum and her colleagues at the University of Iowa tested more than 23,000 high school students, first in the 10th and again in the 12th grade. They found that self-esteem in 10th grade is only weakly predictive of academic achievement in 12th grade. Academic achievement in 10th grade correlates with self-esteem in 12th grade only trivially better. Such results, which are now available from multiple studies, certainly do not indicate that raising self-esteem offers students much benefit. Some findings even suggest that artificially boosting self-esteem may lower subsequent performance.

Even if raising self-esteem does not foster academic progress, might it serve some purpose later, say, on the job? Apparently not. Studies of possible links between workers' self-regard and job performance echo what has been found with schoolwork: the simple search for correlations yields some suggestive results, but these do not show whether a good self-image leads to occupational success, or vice versa. In any case, the link is not particularly strong.

The failure to contribute significantly at school or at the office would be easily offset if a heightened sense of self-worth helped someone to get along better with others. Having a good self-image might make someone more likable insofar as people prefer to associate with confident, positive individuals and generally avoid those who suffer from self-doubts and insecurities.

Good Feelings, Good Grades?

I n an attempt to gauge whether high self-esteem leads to good academic performance, researchers surveyed thousands of high school students in their sophomore and senior years. The correlation between self-esteem sophomore year and academic performance senior year proved to be about the same as the correlation between academic performance sophomore year and self-esteem senior year. Thus, it is hard to say that either trait helps the other or whether some third factor gives rise to both high self-esteem and superior achievement.

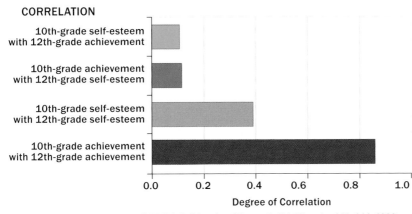

CORRELATION

10th-grade self-esteem with 12th-grade achievement	
10th-grade achievement with 12th-grade self-esteem	
10th-grade self-esteem with 12th-grade self-esteem	
10th-grade achievement with 12th-grade achievement	

0.0 0.2 0.4 0.6 0.8 1.0
Degree of Correlation

SOURCE: S. M. Pottebaum, T. Z. Keith and S. W. Ehly in Educational Research, Vol. 79, pages 140–144; 1986

STONE+

Initiating Relationships

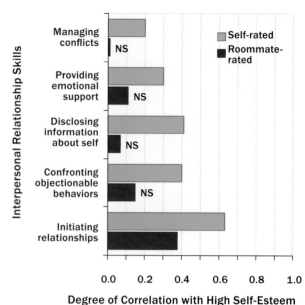

SOURCE: D. Buhrmester, W. Furman, M. T. Wittenberg and H. T. Reis in
Journal of Personality and Social Psychology, Vol. 55, pages 991–1008; 1988

A study of college students revealed strong links between self-esteem and various interpersonal skills—when the subjects rated themselves. Ratings by their roommates provided a different picture: for four of the five skills surveyed, the correlations with self-esteem fell to levels that were not significant (NS) statistically. Nevertheless, the connection between self-esteem and prowess in initiating relationships stayed reasonably robust, as one might expect.

People who regard themselves highly generally state that they are popular and rate their friendships as being of superior quality to those described by people with low self-esteem, who report more negative interactions and less social support. But as Julia Bishop and Heidi M. Inderbitzen-Nolan of the University of Nebraska–Lincoln showed in 1995, these assertions do not reflect reality. The investigators asked 542 ninth-grade students to nominate their most-liked and least-liked peers, and the resulting rankings displayed no correlation whatsoever with self-esteem scores.

A few other sound studies have found that the same is true for adults. In one of these investigations, conducted in the late 1980s, Duane P. Buhrmester, now at the University of Texas at Dallas, reported that college students with high levels of self-regard claimed to be substantially better at initiating relationships, disclosing things about themselves, asserting themselves in response to objectionable behaviors by others, providing emo-

tional support and even managing interpersonal conflicts. Their roommates' ratings, however, told a different story. For four of the five interpersonal skills surveyed, the correlation with self-esteem dropped to near zero. The only one that remained statistically significant was with the subjects' ability to initiate new social contacts and friendships. This does seem to be one sphere in which confidence indeed matters: people who think that they are desirable and attractive should be adept at striking up conversations with strangers, whereas those with low self-esteem presumably shy away, fearing rejection.

One can imagine that such differences might influence a person's love life, too. In 2002 Sandra L. Murray of the University at Buffalo found that people low in self-esteem tend to distrust their partners' expressions of love and support, acting as though they are constantly expecting rejection. Thus far, however, investigators have not produced evidence that such relationships are especially prone to dissolve. In fact, high self-esteem may be the bigger threat: as Caryl E. Rusbult of the University of Kentucky showed back in 1987, those who think highly of themselves are more likely than others to respond to problems by severing relations and seeking other partners.

Sex, Drugs and Rock 'n' Roll

How about teenagers? How does self-esteem, or the lack thereof, influence their love life, in particular their sexual activity? Investigators have

(The Authors)

ROY F. BAUMEISTER, JENNIFER D. CAMPBELL, JOACHIM I. KRUEGER and KATHLEEN D. VOHS collaborated on a more technical paper on self-esteem published in *Psychological Science in the Public Interest* [see "Further Reading," on page 57]. Baumeister is Eppes Professor of Psychology at Florida State University. Campbell, formerly professor of psychology at the University of British Columbia in Vancouver, lives in Florida. Krueger is professor of psychology at Brown University. Vohs is assistant professor of marketing and logistics management at the University of Minnesota.

examined this subject extensively. All in all, the results do not support the idea that low self-esteem predisposes young people to more or earlier sexual activity. If anything, those with high self-esteem are less inhibited, more willing to disregard risks and more prone to engage in sex. At the same time, bad sexual experiences and unwanted pregnancies appear to lower self-esteem.

If not sex, then how about alcohol or illicit drugs? Abuse of these substances is one of the most worrisome behaviors among young people, and many psychologists once believed that boosting self-esteem would prevent such problems. The thought was that people with low self-esteem turn to drinking or drugs for solace. The data, however, do not consistently show that low adolescent self-esteem causes or even correlates with the abuse of alcohol or other drugs. In particular, in a large-scale study in 2000, Rob McGee and Sheila M. Williams of the Dunedin School of Medicine at the University of Otago in New Zealand found no correlation between self-esteem measured between ages nine and 13 and drinking or drug use at age 15. Even when findings do show links between alcohol use and self-esteem, they are mixed and inconclusive. We did find, however, some evidence that low self-esteem contributes to illicit drug use. In particular, Judy A. Andrews and Su-

Mixed Messages

A 1999 study by Donelson R. Forsyth and Natalie A. Kerr, both then at Virginia Commonwealth University, suggests that attempts to boost self-esteem among struggling students may backfire. College students getting grades of D or F in a psychology course were divided into two groups, arranged initially to have the same grade-point average. Each week students in the first group received an e-mail message designed to boost their self-esteem (*example at left*). Those in the second group received a message intended to instill a sense of personal responsibility for their academic performance (*right*).

By the end of the course, the average grade in the first group dropped below 50 percent—a failing grade. The average for students in the second group was 62 percent—a D minus, which is poor but still passing.

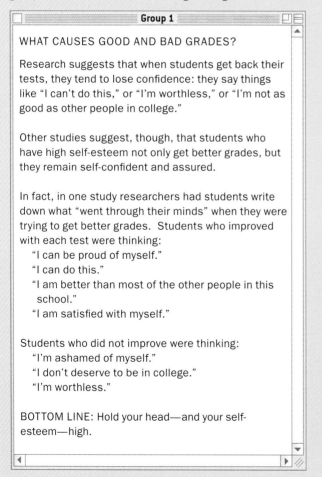

Group 1

WHAT CAUSES GOOD AND BAD GRADES?

Research suggests that when students get back their tests, they tend to lose confidence: they say things like "I can't do this," or "I'm worthless," or "I'm not as good as other people in college."

Other studies suggest, though, that students who have high self-esteem not only get better grades, but they remain self-confident and assured.

In fact, in one study researchers had students write down what "went through their minds" when they were trying to get better grades. Students who improved with each test were thinking:
  "I can be proud of myself."
  "I can do this."
  "I am better than most of the other people in this school."
  "I am satisfied with myself."

Students who did not improve were thinking:
  "I'm ashamed of myself."
  "I don't deserve to be in college."
  "I'm worthless."

BOTTOM LINE: Hold your head—and your self-esteem—high.

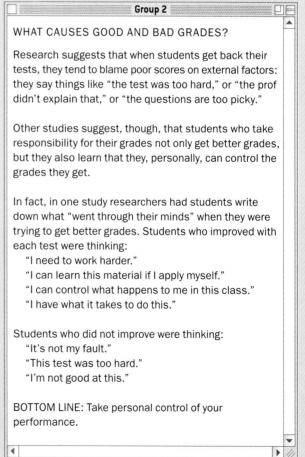

Group 2

WHAT CAUSES GOOD AND BAD GRADES?

Research suggests that when students get back their tests, they tend to blame poor scores on external factors: they say things like "the test was too hard," or "the prof didn't explain that," or "the questions are too picky."

Other studies suggest, though, that students who take responsibility for their grades not only get better grades, but they also learn that they, personally, can control the grades they get.

In fact, in one study researchers had students write down what "went through their minds" when they were trying to get better grades. Students who improved with each test were thinking:
  "I need to work harder."
  "I can learn this material if I apply myself."
  "I can control what happens to me in this class."
  "I have what it takes to do this."

Students who did not improve were thinking:
  "It's not my fault."
  "This test was too hard."
  "I'm not good at this."

BOTTOM LINE: Take personal control of your performance.

san C. Duncan of the Oregon Research Institute found in 1997 that declining levels of academic motivation (the main focus of their study) caused self-esteem to drop, which in turn led to marijuana use, although the connection was weak.

Interpretation of the findings on drinking and drug abuse is probably complicated by the fact that some people approach the experience out of curiosity or thrill seeking, whereas others may use it to cope with or escape from chronic unhappiness. The overall result is that no categorical statements can be made. The same is true for tobacco use, where our study-by-study review uncovered a preponderance of results that show no influence. The few positive findings we unearthed could conceivably reflect nothing more than self-report bias.

Another complication that also clouds these studies is that the category of people with high self-esteem contains individuals whose self-opinions differ in important ways. Yet in most analyses, people with a healthy sense of self-respect are, for example, lumped with those feigning higher self-esteem than they really feel or who are narcissistic. Not surprisingly, the results of such investigations may produce weak or contradictory findings.

Bully for You

For decades, psychologists believed that low self-esteem was an important cause of aggression. One of us (Baumeister) challenged that notion in 1996, when he reviewed assorted studies and concluded that perpetrators of aggression

Self-Esteem and Happiness

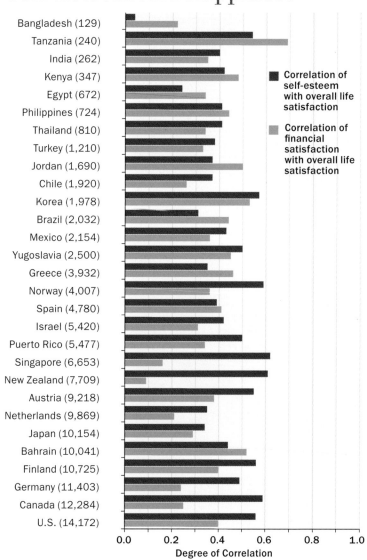

Bangladesh (129)
Tanzania (240)
India (262)
Kenya (347)
Egypt (672)
Philippines (724)
Thailand (810)
Turkey (1,210)
Jordan (1,690)
Chile (1,920)
Korea (1,978)
Brazil (2,032)
Mexico (2,154)
Yugoslavia (2,500)
Greece (3,932)
Norway (4,007)
Spain (4,780)
Israel (5,420)
Puerto Rico (5,477)
Singapore (6,653)
New Zealand (7,709)
Austria (9,218)
Netherlands (9,869)
Japan (10,154)
Bahrain (10,041)
Finland (10,725)
Germany (11,403)
Canada (12,284)
U.S. (14,172)

■ Correlation of self-esteem with overall life satisfaction

▧ Correlation of financial satisfaction with overall life satisfaction

Degree of Correlation

0.0   0.2   0.4   0.6   0.8   1.0

SOURCE: E. Diener and M. Diener in Journal of Personality and Social Psychology, Vol. 68, pages 653–663; 1995

A person's overall satisfaction with life tends to go hand in hand with his or her level of self-esteem, as shown by the high degree of correlation between the two. In most countries overall life satisfaction correlates better with self-esteem than with financial satisfaction. Exceptions tend to be countries with low per capita GDP (*bracketed values, U.S. dollars*).

MELISSA SZALKOWSKI

generally hold favorable and perhaps even inflated views of themselves.

Take the bullying that goes on among children, a common form of aggression. Dan Olweus of the University of Bergen was one of the first to dispute the notion that under their tough exteriors, bullies suffer from insecurities and self-doubts. Although Olweus did not measure self-esteem directly, he showed that bullies reported less anxiety and were more sure of themselves than other children. Apparently the same applies to violent adults [see "Further Reading," below].

After coming to the conclusion that high self-esteem does not lessen a tendency toward violence, that it does not deter adolescents from turning to alcohol, tobacco, drugs and sex, and that it fails to improve academic or job performance, we got a boost when we looked into how self-esteem relates to happiness. The consistent finding is that people with high self-esteem are significantly happier than others. They are also less likely to be depressed.

One especially compelling study was published in 1995, after Diener and his daughter Marissa, now a psychologist at the University of Utah, surveyed more than 13,000 college students, and high self-esteem emerged as the strongest factor in overall life satisfaction. In 2004 Sonja Lyubomirsky, Christopher Tkach and M. Robin DiMatteo of the University of California, Riverside, reported data from more than 600 adults ranging in age from 51 to 95. Once again, happiness and self-esteem proved to be closely tied. Before it is safe to conclude that high self-esteem leads to happiness, however, further research must address the shortcomings of the work that has been done so far.

First, causation needs to be established. It seems possible that high self-esteem brings about happiness, but no research has shown this outcome. The strong correlation between self-esteem and happiness is just that—a correlation. It is plausible that occupational, academic or interpersonal successes cause both happiness and high self-esteem and that corresponding failures cause both unhappiness and low self-esteem. It is even possible that happiness, in the sense of a temperament or disposition to feel good, induces high self-esteem.

Second, it must be recognized that happiness (and its opposite, depression) has been studied mainly by means of self-report, and the tendency of some people toward negativity may produce both their low opinions of themselves and unfavorable evaluations of other aspects of life. Yet it is not clear what could replace such assessments. An investigator would indeed be hard-pressed to demonstrate convincingly that a person was less (or more) happy than he or she supposed. Clearly, objective measures of happiness and depression are going to be difficult if not impossible to obtain, but that does not mean self-reports should be accepted uncritically.

What then should we do? Should parents, teachers and therapists seek to boost self-esteem wherever possible? In the course of our literature review, we found some indications that self-esteem is a helpful attribute. It improves persistence in the face of failure. And individuals with high self-esteem sometimes perform better in groups than do those with low self-esteem. Also, a poor self-image is a risk factor for certain eating disorders, especially bulimia—a connection one of us (Vohs) and her colleagues documented in 1999. Other effects are harder to demonstrate with objective evidence, although we are inclined to accept the subjective evidence that self-esteem goes hand in hand with happiness.

So we can certainly understand how an injection of self-esteem might be valuable to the individual. But imagine if a heightened sense of self-worth prompted some people to demand preferential treatment or to exploit their fellows. Such tendencies would entail considerable social costs. And we have found little to indicate that indiscriminately promoting self-esteem in today's children or adults, just for being themselves, offers society any compensatory benefits beyond the seductive pleasure it brings to those engaged in the exercise. **M**

Young people with high self-esteem are more prone to disregard risks and engage in sex.

(Further Reading)

◆ **Violent Pride.** Roy F. Baumeister in *Scientific American,* Vol. 284, No. 4, pages 96–101; April 2001.
◆ **Does High Self-Esteem Cause Better Performance, Interpersonal Success, Happiness, or Healthier Lifestyles?** Roy F. Baumeister, Jennifer D. Campbell, Joachim I. Krueger and Kathleen D. Vohs in *Psychological Science in the Public Interest,* Vol. 4, No. 1, pages 1–44; May 2003.

The
Medicated
Americans

Close to 10 percent of men and women in America are now taking drugs to combat depression. How did a once rare condition become so common?

By Charles Barber

Adapted from *Comfortably Numb: How Psychiatry Is Medicating a Nation*, by Charles Barber (Pantheon Books, 2008).

I am thinking of the Medicated Americans, those 11 percent of women and 5 percent of men who are taking antidepressants.

It is Sunday night. The Medicated American—let's call her Julie, and let's place her in Winterset, Iowa—is getting ready for bed. Monday morning and its attendant pressures—the rush to get out of the house, the long commute, the bustle of the office—loom. She opens the cabinet of the bathroom vanity, removes a medicine bottle and taps a pill into her palm. She fills a glass of water, places the colorful pill in her mouth and swallows. The little pill could be any one of 30 available drugs used as antidepressants—such as Prozac or Zoloft or Paxil or Celexa or Lexapro or Luvox or Buspar or Nardil or Elavil or Sinequan or Pamelor or Serzone or Desyrel or Norpramin or Tofranil or Adapin or Vivactil or Ludiomil or Endep or Parnate or Remeron. The pill makes a slight flutter as it passes down her throat.

Julie examines her face in the mirror and sighs. She hopes that by some Monday morning in the future—if not tomorrow morning, then some mythical, brilliant and shimmering Monday morning a month from now, or two months from now, or three—the pills will have worked some kind of inexorable magic. Corrected a chemical imbalance, or something, as the Zoloft commercial had said. "Zoloft, a prescription medicine, can help. It works to correct chemical imbalances in the brain," the voiceover on the ad had intoned. Julie didn't know she had a chemical imbalance, nor does she actually know what one is, and it had never really occurred to her that she could have a mental illness (could she?). But she does hope, fervently, that her life will become a little easier, a little less stressed—soon. She hopes, desperately, that the pills will make her feel better—that the little white powder hidden in the green capsule will dissolve in her stomach, enter her bloodstream, travel to her brain and do something. Brushing her teeth, she hopes that one day she will simply feel better.

Mental Illness by the Numbers

If statistics serve, we know a number of things about the Medicated American. We know there is a very good chance she has no psychiatric diagnosis. A study of antidepressant use in private health insurance plans by the New England Research Institute found that 43 percent of those who had been prescribed antidepressants had no psychiatric diagnosis or any mental health care beyond the prescription of the drug. We know she is probably female: twice as many psychiatric drugs are prescribed for women than for men, reported a 1991 study in the *British Journal of Psychiatry*. Remarkably, in 2002 more than one in three doctor's office visits by women involved the prescription of an antidepressant, either for the writing of a new prescription or for the maintenance of an existing one, according to the Centers for Disease Control and Prevention.

We know that most likely a psychiatrist did not prescribe her antidepressants: family doctors

frequently now prescribe such medications. We know that Julie in Iowa was far more likely to ask her doctor for an antidepressant after having seen it advertised on TV or in print; one fifth of Americans have asked their doctor for a drug after they have seen it advertised. And when Julie asked for her antidepressant, her doctor was likely to comply with the request, even if he or she felt ambivalent about the choice of drug or diagnosis.

It is unlikely that the doctor spent much time talking to Julie about the nature of the drugs, the common side-effect profiles and the remote but potentially dangerous side effects. Based on taped sessions, a 2006 study at the University of California, Los Angeles, showed that when prescribing a new medicine, two thirds of doctors said nothing to the patient about how long to take the medication, and almost half did not indicate the dosage amount and frequency. Only about a third of the time did doctors talk about adverse side effects. In the case of antidepressants, failure to review possible side effects and to monitor the patient's progress in the weeks and months after starting the drugs is deeply irresponsible. A 2004 study in the *Journal of the American Medical Association* stated that "the

risk of suicidal behavior is increased in the first month after starting antidepressants, especially during the first one to nine days." Worse, there is no longer any need to deal with an actual physician: all these drugs are readily available, with a few clicks and a credit card.

We further know that Julie's managed care insurance was more than happy to cover the prescription, especially if it meant that the company did not have to pay for therapy, which Julie is less and less likely, and less and less able, to pursue—an unsurprising fact given that there are only about 40,000 psychiatrists in the country. As a result, after starting antidepressants and taking them for three months, three quarters of adults and more than half of children do not see a doctor or therapist specifically for mental heath care, found a study by Medco Health Solutions. Another report, referenced in the *New York Times*, reported that only 20 percent of people who take antidepressants have any kind of follow-up appointment to monitor the medication.

Between 1987 and 1997, while the rate of pharmacological treatment for depression doubled, the number of psychotherapy visits for depression decreased, as cited in a study in the Jan-

Diagnosis confusion: If she were actually experiencing severe depression, she couldn't have summoned the energy to get to the party.

(Julie's managed care insurance was **more than happy** to cover the prescription.)

A clinically depressed person may not be able to drag herself out of bed.

uary 9, 2002, issue of the *Journal of the American Medical Association*. These days only about 3 percent of the population receives therapy from a psychiatrist, psychologist or social worker, according to a 2006 study in *Archives of General Psychiatry*. The strong likelihood is that the fluttering of the pill down her throat will be the extent of Julie's mental health treatment.

A Growing Trend

Antidepressant SSRIs (selective serotonin reuptake inhibitors) were first approved as treatment for clinical depression, and other uses were steadily added during the 1990s: indications came, one after the other, for obsessive-compulsive disorder, eating disorders, anxiety and premenstrual dysphoric disorder. The drugs were also used for paraphilias, sexual compulsions and body dysmorphic disorder. With each new utilization, the market got bigger, lines between distress and disease got blurrier, and the drugs began to be prescribed for problems beyond those indicated by the Food and Drug Administration. As a result, a good number of Americans are now taking SSRIs for non-FDA-approved uses, termed "off label" prescriptions. A 2006 study found that three quarters of people prescribed antidepressant drugs receive the medications for a reason not approved by the FDA. This practice is legal and intended to give physicians the flexibility to prescribe the drugs that are best

suited to their patients' needs. The problem is that "most off-label drug mentions have little or no scientific support," says study co-author Jack Fincham of the University of Georgia College of Pharmacy. "And when I say most, it's like 70 to 75 percent. Many patients have no idea that this goes on and just assume that the physician is writing a prescription for their indication."

So, if not for a severe mental illness, why exactly is Julie taking the antidepressants? One reason traces to the existence of the catchall term "depression." Depression, once considered a rare disease usually associated with elderly women, is overwhelmingly the mental health diagnosis of choice of our time. About 40 percent of mental health complaints result in its diagnosis, according to the CDC. Martin E. P. Seligman of the University of Pennsylvania, perhaps America's most influential academic psychologist, has stated: "If you're born around World War I, in your lifetime the prevalence of depression, severe depression, is about 1 percent. If you're born around World War II, the lifetime prevalence of depression seemed to be about 5 percent. If you were born starting in the 1960s, the lifetime prevalence seemed to be between 10 and 15 percent, and this is with lives incomplete." (When entire life spans are ultimately taken into account, the rate could grow further.) Moreover, Seligman notes, the age of onset of the first depressive episode has dropped. A generation or two ago the onset of depression purportedly occurred on average at age 34 or 35; recent studies have found the mean age for the first bout of depression to be 14 years old.

It is as if from the early 1990s on (nicely coinciding with the mass penetration of Prozac), we have been living in the Age of Depression—just as Valium arrived in, or helped to create, the Age of Anxiety. In contemporary America, it has been broadly accepted for some time that everybody, at some level, is depressed at least some of the time. As Americans have become more aware of their

One feels such patients' anguish at a primal, physiological level. "Very often patients with major depression will say the emotional pain they feel is worse than the pain of any physical illness," said J. John Mann, chief of neuroscience at the New York Psychiatric Institute, in a 1997 article in *BrainWork*. Many depressed people really, really want to die, and thinking about dying, or planning their death, takes up a great deal of their time. So horrific is the incapacitation that the highest risk of suicide actually comes when

(In contemporary America, it is broadly accepted that **everybody is depressed** at least some of the time.)

feelings in the past few therapy-oriented decades, it has become acceptable and eminently appropriate to say when someone asks how you are feeling (particularly if it's late March): "A little depressed." Or to respond to the query, "How was the movie the other day?": "A little depressing." Or to say in response to "How did you feel about last year's minuscule raise?": "Depressed."

But to anyone reasonably experienced in the mental health field, there is depression and then there is Depression. The first type is a terribly broad and bland term, indicating "the blues," "feeling down," "bummed out," "in the dumps," "low," "a little tired," "not quite myself," each a standard part of the daily human predicament. Major depressive disorder, however, is a harrowing and indisputably profound and serious medical condition. To confuse the two, depression with Depression, is to compare a gentle spring rain to a vengeful typhoon.

A true diagnosis of major depression involves some combination of most of the following: inability to feel pleasure of any kind whatsoever, loss of interest in everything, extreme self-hatred or guilt, inability to concentrate or to do the simplest things, sleeping all the time or not being able to sleep at all, dramatic weight gain or loss, and wanting to kill yourself or actually trying to kill yourself. Truly depressed people do not smile or laugh; they may not talk; they are not fun to be with; they do not wish to be visited; they may not eat and have to be fed with feeding tubes so as not to die; and they exude a palpable and monstrous sense of pain. It is a thing unto itself, an undeniably physical and medical affliction and *not*, as psychiatrist Paul McHugh writes, "just the dark side of human emotion."

people are feeling slightly better. In the throes of an episode, depressed patients are too dissipated to even muster the energy to kill themselves. I thought I knew the difference between the blues and major depression until I saw the disease in its full and malicious force. The only treatments are hospitalization, supervision, rest, quiet, sedatives, sleep medications, an appropriate level of antidepressants and electroshock therapy. Despite its side effects (such as short-term memory loss), electroshock therapy remains the single most effective treatment for major depression.

Dicey Diagnosis

What modern psychiatry has done, I am convinced, is to conflate and confuse the two, Depression and depression. David Healy, in *Let Them Eat Prozac* (NYU Press, 2004), calls it "a creation of depression on so extraordinary and unwarranted a scale as to raise questions about whether pharmaceutical and other health care companies are more wedded to making profits from health than contributing to it." A 2007 study at New York University showed that about one in four people who appears to be depressed and is treated as such is in fact dealing with the aftermath of a recent emotional blow, such as the end of a marriage, the loss of a job or the collapse of a business.

Each successive edition of the *Diagnostic and Statistical Manual of Mental Disorders* (DSM) has proclaimed an ever increasing number of di-

(The Author)

CHARLES BARBER is a psychiatry lecturer at the Yale University School of Medicine.

agnoses that cover an ever widening terrain of normal, if painful, human behavior. *DSM-I,* published in 1952, covered some 150 diagnoses. *DSM-IV,* which came out in the 1990s, had more than 350. The next version, *DSM-V,* due in 2011, will introduce even more.

In contrast, large percentages of people with severe and persistent mental illness get no care whatsoever. "The majority of those with a diagnosable mental disorder [are] not receiving treatment," wrote the U.S. surgeon general in a 1999 report. Studies published in 1985, 2000 and 2001 found that 50, 42 and 46 percent, respectively, of people with serious mental illness were receiving no treatment for their conditions. A massive study in the early 2000s on the prevalence of mental illness led by health care policy researcher Ronald C. Kessler of Harvard Medical School, in collaboration with the World Health Organization, revealed that in developed countries 35 to 50 percent of people with serious cases had not been treated in the previous year; in poor countries the figure was 80 percent. A separate study, published in 2002, found that of those in the U.S. receiving treatment for serious mental illness, only 40 percent were receiving what is considered minimally adequate treatment. Of all those with serious mental disorders, then, only 15 percent were getting the high-quality care they needed.

The same tragic imbalance exists in the research world. Although people with severe mental illness account for more than half of the direct costs associated with all mental illness, only about a third of National Institute of Mental Health research awards from 1997 to 2002 went to the study of serious mental illness.

The slippery slope that psychiatry has traversed—jettisoning the impoverished mentally ill for the cash-carrying worried well—can perhaps be traced to a single word choice in *DSM-III,* the totally revised diagnostic manual of 1980. But not for the selection of that one word, the recent history of psychiatry might be entirely different.

The prevailing term to describe specific psychiatric conditions in *DSM-I* in 1952 was an odd one: "reaction." Schizophrenia, for example, was described as a "schizophrenic reaction." Depression was a "depressive reaction." The concept of "reaction" derived from psychoanalytic thinking, and, as such, mental torment was thought to come about as a result of a reaction to environmental, psychological and biological problems. By *DSM-II,* in 1968, the term "reaction" had been tossed aside. *DSM-II* described depression in more psychological terms such as depressive neurosis and depressive psychosis.

DSM-III, which was the brainchild of one man, Robert Spitzer of Columbia, was an attempt to strike a middle ground between the psychoanalytic camp, which had no interest in biology, and the budding brain scientists, who were starting to gain traction as psychiatric drugs were becoming more prevalent and often successfully treating people with severe mental illness. Spitzer, who is probably, after Sigmund Freud, the most influential psychiatrist of the 20th century, worked on *DSM-III* for six years, often up to 80 hours a week. To appease both groups, Spitzer brought a centrist, "theory-neutral" approach to his work. He based diagnoses not on theories and traditions about how they might have arisen but on objective observation and symptom lists, on

Antidepressants may be the only mental health therapy many patients receive.

Pharmaceutical remedies have expanded along with diagnoses for new "disorders."

the "here and now." Although this strategy was no doubt well intentioned, the lack of theoretical constraint meant that just about any painful and unhappy human predicament could be entertained for inclusion.

Spitzer presided over an extraordinary expansion of the *DSM*. "Bob never met a new diagnosis that he didn't at least get interested in," said Allen Frances, a psychiatrist who worked closely with Spitzer on *DSM-III*, in a 2005 interview with the *New Yorker*. "Anything, however against his own leanings that might be, was a new thing to play with, a new toy." Spitzer was a technician of diagnosis and loved to compose symptom lists, sometimes drawing them up on the spot. It should be noted that in his centrist approach, Spitzer also presided over many positive developments. For example, he removed homosexuality as a diagnosis, which had been notoriously included in *DSM-II*. Spitzer also excised "hysterical personality" disorder—which had become unfairly identified with female instability. (The word "hysteria" itself comes from "uterus"—hence the term "hysterectomy.")

The word that Spitzer settled on, to cover the vast majority of all the roughly 300 diagnoses, was "disorder." "Disorder" was not entirely new: it had appeared briefly in earlier editions of the *DSM* to describe general categories of distress. The problem is that "disorder," so bland and toothless, so appeasing to all parties, has little meaning. There are few constraints on the word "disorder." Just about everything can be a disorder.

Spitzer's word choice created the slippery slope that psychiatry occupies today. Had Spitzer settled on, say, the word "disease" instead, it is conceivable that the course of modern psychiatry would have been different. Diseases are scary, upsetting, painful, often chronic and potentially lethal. You stay in bed with diseases. People do not like to be around you when you have a disease. You generally do not look well when you have a disease.

I think we have got to get beyond the absurd vapidity of disorder categories such as "phase of life problem" and "sibling relational problem." We should get a little more specific about Julie's angst. Let us take the daring step of calling life problems what they are and what they were up until about 20 years ago: life problems. **M**

(Further Reading)

◆ **Blaming the Brain: The Truth about Drugs and Mental Health.** Eliot S. Valenstein. The Free Press, 2000.
◆ **Of Two Minds: An Anthropologist Looks at American Psychiatry.** T. M. Luhrmann. Alfred A. Knopf, 2000.
◆ **Let Them Eat Prozac.** David Healy. NYU Press, 2004.

COMBATING STRESS IN IRAQ

Psychologists on the battlefield are helping soldiers stay mentally fit during long and frightful tours of duty

Bret A. Moore and
Greg M. Reger

A U.S. Army soldier peers through the window of his Humvee in Tikrit, Iraq, after it was hit by a home-made bomb.

uring a routine patrol outside a small village in eastern Iraq, a four-vehicle convoy was suddenly blasted with an improvised explosive device (IED). Michael (not his real name), a 22-year-old combat medic who was riding in one of the vehicles, lost consciousness for several moments. As he regained his senses, he saw that the gunner had been thrown from the turret. Michael immediately scrambled out of the mangled vehicle and began to apply first aid. After stabilizing the injured soldier, Michael proceeded to the next truck ahead to see if there were further casualties. As he approached, a second IED detonated. Michael was knocked out again. When he came to, he saw that the driver was seriously injured. Michael gave him CPR and struggled over him for 10 minutes, but the man died in his arms.

Two days later, as part of the routine follow-up to such an incident, a psychologist with the unit's combat stress control team conducted a debriefing of the members of the convoy. Throughout the discussion Michael was quiet and reserved, showing no emotion. Then, six days later, he appeared at the psychologist's quarters and reported that he was having trouble sleeping, was experiencing nightmares, had lost his appetite and had an intense fear of going on future missions.

The psychologist promptly initiated treatment for Michael, assuring him that what he was experiencing was to be expected. The therapist taught him behavioral techniques that would help him sleep, facilitated a brief course of sleep medication, and educated him on the importance of maintaining a regular exercise and work routine. The psychologist also started Michael on daily therapy sessions, and he was placed on restricted duty for the next seven days. At the end of that time Michael reported that he could sleep better and was clear of nightmares. He regained his appetite as well as his confidence in his abilities as a soldier and a medic. The unit's commander placed Michael back on full-mission status, and he continued with his military duties.

Army psychologists are playing a critical role in maintaining the emotional and psychological well-being of service members in Iraq. Their ability to get to the troops quickly and treat them on the battlefield is making a difference in how well our fighting men and women are able to deal with the potentially disabling consequences of combat stress. Michael's story highlights the toll that combat exposure can take, and it illustrates how prompt and targeted intervention can mitigate the present and possible future effects of traumatic experiences. The case also illustrates the tactical and operational importance of the army psychologist in Iraq. Helping emotionally stressed service members return to their prior level of functioning is not only the best medicine for their mental health, it is key to a military unit retaining valuable soldiers, which is crucial to operational success.

Unable to Function

Traditionally, the human cost of war has been viewed primarily through physical lenses. Talk of combat casualties usually refers to physical injury or death on the battlefield. Yet the emotional and psychological effects of combat on service members can also be devastating. It can even be the critical factor in whether or not a military force is successful.

The first accounts of combat stress on warriors can be traced back to early mythology. But it was not until the 17th century that military leaders began to realize that the stress on soldiers could have a profound influence on the success of military operations. The condition was originally called "Swiss disease," because doctors and leaders in the Swiss Army noted that some men no longer had the motivation or ability to continue fighting. Many would just give up

JACK WHITE, ARMY STAFF SGT., 116TH BCT PUBLIC AFFAIRS (top); LEK MATEO, ARMY MASTER SGT., 56TH BCT PUBLIC AFFAIRS (bottom)

or become so incapacitated by fear that they could not physically function. Over the next centuries this phenomenon went through several name changes, including nostalgia, irritable heart, shell shock, battle fatigue and the current designation of combat stress reaction.

Combat stress may arise when an event, situation or condition in a fighting zone requires a soldier to alter his or her behavior in response to new demands. The change typically presents cognitive, physiological and emotional challenges. Such stress is a normal and expected experience for deployed personnel, and the vast majority of soldiers manage it effectively. Many actually perform better under reasonable levels of stress. But certain situations can place so much strain on an individual that he or she cannot maintain a normal level of functioning. Emotionally, a service member suffering from a combat stress reaction may exhibit sadness, worry, fear or even inappropriate euphoria. Cognitively, the person may experience disorientation, confusion, memory loss or inattention. And behaviorally, he or she may exhibit an increase in aggressive or suicidal behavior. In extreme cases, the service member could potentially engage in hostile behavior toward local civilians or enemy detainees.

We should note that the term "post-traumatic stress disorder," or PTSD, is often used to de-

scribe a service member's reaction to battlefield events. PTSD is a specific psychiatric diagnosis, however, characterized by emotional trouble months or years after trauma. A combat stress reaction may or may not lead to the development of this disorder.

Soldiers in Iraq are affected by the same problems that military personnel over the centuries have been forced to endure. Still, for the American troops currently deployed overseas, two important differences can further impinge on their psychological health. First, at no other

Author Bret Moore (*top center*) discusses stress with soldiers at their compound in Iraq. Author Greg Reger (*bottom*) stands before an armored vehicle that medical personnel use on the battlefield.

> # The anxiety of knowing that an attack can occur anywhere, anytime, can be difficult to manage.

Personnel who cannot shake fear after being treated at their camp may be sent to a base that has more extensive therapeutic resources.

time in American military history have service members been required to take such a defensive and reactive posture in combat operations. Although the initial assault on Baghdad in the early months of 2003 and the retaking of Fallujah in November 2004 were aggressive operations, much of the troops' time is spent patrolling villages, convoying between forward operating bases and searching for unexploded IEDs. The anxiety and fear of not knowing if or when an attack might occur can be difficult to manage. Second, everyone is in harm's way. The days of the soldier with the "gear in the rear" are over. There is no more "front line"; the linear battlefield has given way to self-supporting bases and camps strategically scattered throughout the region. Many support troops who would have been spared the emotional strains of combat in previous wars are now as vulnerable as the infantrymen. Consequently, larger numbers of combat stress casualties are possible. Fortunately, the military has recognized these changes and the potential problems that may arise. It has gone to great lengths to increase the number of mental health providers in Iraq. Army psychologists and combat stress control teams have become important operational assets.

Little Time to Talk

When asked to describe a psychologist, the public often imagines an older middle-aged man with a graying beard, probably with a cigar and

(The Authors)

BRET A. MOORE and GREG M. REGER are captains in the U.S. Army and met two years ago during training. Moore (bret.moore@us.army.mil) is a clinical and aeromedical psychologist with the 85th Combat Stress Control Unit, based in Fort Hood, Tex. He is currently deployed in Kirkuk, Iraq, where he is the officer in charge of a CSC preventive team. Reger is a clinical and aeromedical psychologist with the 98th Combat Stress Control Unit, based in Fort Lewis, Wash. He is deployed in Tallil, Iraq, where he is a psychologist with a CSC restoration team. Moore and Reger wrote a chapter on combat stress for the upcoming book *For Those Who Bore the Battle: Combat Stress Injury Theory, Research, and Management*, edited by C. R. Figley and W. P. Nash (Routledge, 2006). The views expressed here are those of the authors and do not reflect the official position of the U.S. Army, U.S. Department of Defense or U.S. government.

LEK MATEO, ARMY MASTER SGT., 56TH BCT PUBLIC AFFAIRS

A Soldier First

It was late on a Tuesday afternoon when the platoon sergeant stopped by my makeshift office. Because of a recent increase in activity among nearby Iraqi insurgents, the platoon would be conducting traffic checkpoints that night in a densely populated city in northern Iraq. Concerned about his men, the sergeant asked me, the psychologist deployed to support his platoon, to accompany the unit so I could observe his soldiers. He wanted to know if stress was adversely affecting their performance. I had been on missions before, but none with this much potential exposure to enemy contact. Nevertheless, I agreed to go.

After cordoning off an area in the heart of the city, the unit began to stop and inspect vehicles. Even with temperatures still hovering around 100 degrees Fahrenheit at 11:00 P.M., the traffic was steady and the streets were bustling with bystanders. About an hour into the mission, a small car carrying four young Iraqi men approached. One soldier was at the checkpoint gate with me, and several others were close by. While the soldier was checking identifications, he realized that one of the passengers in the rear seat met the description of a wanted insurgent. As he questioned the suspect, a verbal confrontation ensued, and the two men in the front seats began to exit the car. As instructed in my previous training, I raised my gun and directed it at the men in an aggressive posture. Within seconds four other soldiers from the unit surrounded the vehicle with weapons drawn. A full search turned up several illegal weapons and materials used to make improvised explosive devices. The men were detained and taken to the local Iraqi police station. I breathed a huge sigh of relief.

Unlike in past world wars, today's battlefields do not typically have clearly delineated front lines and somewhat safe support positions in the rear. Violence erupts anywhere at any time. Explosives can be hidden in seemingly innocuous items such as cars, roadside debris and even baby strollers and can be carried by insurgents

To ascertain how stress is affecting behavior, psychologists take part in dangerous assignments and must therefore be reliable soldiers as well.

dressed in civilian clothes. Given this ease of disguise, today's army psychologists may find themselves alongside combat troops in dangerous situations. As a result, the army is reemphasizing the importance of psychologists and all support professionals being proficient not just in their occupational skills but also as soldiers.

I certainly did not relish standing at that checkpoint. But it was necessary for me to observe how stress might be affecting soldiers' actions, and if I had not reacted quickly enough, or had overreacted, my inappropriate actions could have allowed or caused a deadly fight.

Later, I told the sergeant that although his men were experiencing elevated levels of stress, they were still performing their jobs competently and safely. To reach that conclusion, I had to be in the midst of an important tactical operation. Furthermore, by inserting himself or herself in harm's way, a psychologist achieves two other crucial goals. First, the soldiers in a unit may develop a greater sense of trust in the psychologist and therefore be less reluctant to participate in mental health services. And second, the psychologist is better able to appreciate the stress unique to a combat environment, thereby imparting a far deeper understanding of what soldiers experience. —B.A.M.

an Austrian accent, who quietly takes notes alongside a patient who is lying on a couch. This image is as out of place in the army as the Freudian theories associated with it [see box above]. Historically, mental health providers have treated patients from a variety of psychoanalytical or psychodynamic theories that generally conceptualized an individual's problem as stemming from unconscious, repressed thoughts or feelings. Clinicians intervened with long-term talk therapy that attempted to bring this hidden material into consciousness, in hopes of giving the

patient insight into the supposed root of his or her symptoms or finding a corrective experience in therapy.

Even though army psychologists may continue to draw from these theories to conceptualize a soldier's difficulties, the realities of a combat zone make long-term talk therapy impractical. Soldiers' mission schedules are unpredictable. Troop movements and unit reorganizations occur regularly. Psychologists may have only brief access to soldiers traveling through a particular forward operating base. As a result, army psy-

anger may wane. Although psychologists certainly take into account a soldier's environment, background and family history, short-term, non-pharmacological interventions such as cognitive behavioral therapy are the backbone of treatment in a combat zone.

Immediate Attention

The mission of an army combat stress control (CSC) team is straightforward: provide prevention and treatment as close to the soldier's unit as possible, with the intent of keeping the soldier with the group. CSC teams are specialized mobile mental health groups that are typically deployed to distant battlefields. They may supplement existing mental health teams or function independently, depending on the need or battlefield configuration. The development of these unique teams springs from lessons learned from World War I: if combat stress cases were evacuated to the rear, they seldom returned to their units, but when soldiers were treated close to the front, they were more likely to return to duty and less likely to have ongoing mental health problems on their return home.

Among the military's diverse mental health providers—which include psychiatrists, psychiatric nurses, occupational therapists and social workers—psychologists play an integral role in CSC units. We operate under four basic treatment principles: proximity, immediacy, expectancy and simplicity, a scheme known as PIES. Proximity refers to treating the soldier as close to his or her unit as possible. Immediacy acknowledges the importance of intervening as quickly as possible, to mitigate the impact of traumatic events and ward off potential long-term problems. Expectancy means helping the soldier realize that symptoms such as being afraid to go on further missions after being hit with an IED are expected, or typical, reactions to an abnormal situation and that with time these feelings will subside and allow for a full return to duty. Finally, simplicity encompasses the short-term and evidence-based treatment techniques such as cognitive behavioral therapy as well as ensures that the soldier's basic needs of rest, food and hygiene are met.

Psychologists in a CSC unit serve in two main ways: prevention and restoration. Preventive teams are typically found in remote battlefield areas. Their primary responsibilities are working to ward off combat stress, triaging it and setting up short-term treatment if it occurs. A CSC psychologist educates personnel in a va-

A soldier in Baghdad mourns at a memorial service for a 19-year-old compatriot killed when the truck he was riding in was hit by a rocket-propelled grenade.

chologists rely on more recent therapeutic models of short-term treatment.

One approach often employed is cognitive behavioral therapy. This practice recognizes the important role that thinking has on an individual's feelings and behavior. Challenging a person's irrational, illogical or dysfunctional beliefs can alter his or her moods and actions. For example, a soldier who feels angry with other members of the unit may have vindictive thoughts and act in verbally aggressive ways toward them. By recognizing and altering how the person thinks about his or her peers, the intensity and duration of the

DAVID LEESON Dallas Morning News/Corbis Sygma

riety of areas such as how to avoid acting on thoughts of suicide, handling conflicts and reducing stress. In triage, the psychologist may have to travel to an outlying camp that was subjected to a traumatic event to assess and identify soldiers who are having acute stress reactions. At this point, the psychologist can decide whether to initiate a regimen of short-term therapy or

intense fear and feel hopeless about their ultimate survival. He coordinated an air evacuation of the two men to a regional restoration team, where they received more intensive and comprehensive services. Six days later the soldiers were able to return to mission status with their unit. Although some residual fear remained, the two men and their providers judged that the linger-

(Psychologists may have only brief access to soldiers passing through. Treatment must be short-term.)

to refer someone to the restoration team for more extensive care.

Restoration teams are usually located at a base that has greater access to resources than the remote units do. Here a psychologist works with a soldier on a longer-term basis, which in the army may mean anywhere from three days to two weeks. In certain cases, treatment could extend for several months. The soldier may receive daily individual and group therapy and training on stress and anger management, relaxation, and ways to get a better night's rest. Furthermore, the psychologist can help coordinate medication for sleep problems, depression and anxiety, as well as utilize the unique skills of occupational therapists. Prevention and restoration work together:

On his weekly visit to a remote camp that housed several infantry units, a preventive team psychologist learned from a sergeant that three days earlier one soldier was killed and several were seriously injured after an enemy rocket hit the camp's crowded dining facility. The psychologist immediately brought together the personnel who were involved and held a crisis debriefing—a one-time group session that allows everyone to discuss and process what happened.

Over the next several days, the psychologist worked one-on-one with a number of soldiers who were still struggling with the attack. Through individual therapy, coordinating sleep medication with the camp's physician assistant, and placing some of the soldiers on restricted duty to ensure they received adequate rest and recovery, he helped most of the personnel regain the level of functioning that they had before the incident.

The psychologist did identify two soldiers who had begun to suffer panic attacks, develop

ing stress was not sufficient to prevent them from doing their job or to put them or other members of their unit at risk.

The stress of war can have a tremendous impact on a service member. But with targeted and prompt intervention, a psychologist can help mitigate the acute effects of combat stress and, it is hoped, prevent the development of future mental health problems when the soldier returns home. Combat stress can also hurt a military unit as a whole. Without the appropriate level of manpower, the unit may be unable to function optimally, compromising an important military operation and placing many troops at risk.

Fortunately, the military has recognized the importance of ensuring quality mental health care to its members. At a minimum, our country owes these brave men and women a return home to their loved ones and a future not plagued by emotional and psychological problems. We are not so naive as to believe that these warriors will be completely unaffected by their experiences. But by adapting psychological principles common in the civilian sector to the battlefield, psychologists and combat stress control teams can alleviate the damaging effects of the inevitable stresses of war. **M**

(Further Reading)

◆ "Forward Psychiatry" in the Military: Its Origins and Effectiveness. Edgar Jones and Simon Wessely in *Journal of Traumatic Stress,* Vol. 16, No. 4, pages 411–419; August 2003.

◆ A Historical Overview of Combat Stress Control Units of the U.S. Army. Bryan L. Bacon and James J. Staudenmeier in *Military Medicine,* Vol. 168, No. 9, pages 689–693; September 2003.

◆ Stressed Out at the Front. Rod Nordland and T. Trent Gegax in *Newsweek,* Vol. 143, No. 2, pages 34–37; January 12, 2004.

◆ Clinician to Frontline Soldier: A Look at the Roles and Challenges of Army Clinical Psychologists in Iraq. Bret A. Moore and Greg M. Reger in *Journal of Clinical Psychology* (in press).

By Robert B. Cialdini

the SCIENCE of Persuasion

Social psychology has determined the basic principles that govern getting to "yes"

Hello there.

I hope you've enjoyed the magazine so far. Now I'd like to let you in on something of great importance to you personally. Have you ever been tricked into saying yes? Ever felt trapped into buying something you didn't really want or contributing to some suspicious-sounding cause? And have you ever wished you understood why you acted in this way so that you could withstand these clever ploys in the future?

Yes? Then clearly this article is just right for you. It contains valuable information on the most powerful psychological pressures that get you to say yes to requests. And it's chock-full of NEW, IMPROVED research showing exactly how and why these techniques work. So don't delay, just settle in and get the information that, after all, you've already agreed you want.

The scientific study of the process of social influence has been under way for well over half a century, beginning in earnest with the propaganda, public information and persuasion programs of World War II. Since that time, numerous social scientists have investigated the ways in which one individual can influence another's attitudes and actions. For the past 30 years, I have participated in that endeavor, concentrating primarily on the major factors that bring about a specific form of behavior change—compliance with a request. Six basic tendencies of human behavior come into play in generating a positive response: recip-rocation, consistency, social validation, liking, authority and scarcity. As these six tendencies help to govern our business dealings, our societal involvements and our personal relationships, knowledge of the rules of persuasion can truly be thought of as empowerment.

Reciprocation

When the Disabled American Veterans organization mails out requests for contributions, the appeal succeeds only about 18 percent of the time. But when the mailing includes a set of free personalized address labels, the success rate almost doubles, to 35 percent. To understand the effect of

the unsolicited gift, we must recognize the reach and power of an essential rule of human conduct: the code of reciprocity.

All societies subscribe to a norm that obligates individuals to repay in kind what they have received. Evolutionary selection pressure has probably entrenched the behavior in social animals such as ourselves. The demands of reciprocity begin to explain the boost in donations to the veterans group. Receiving a gift—unsolicited and perhaps even unwanted—convinced significant numbers of potential donors to return the favor.

Charitable organizations are far from alone in taking this approach: food stores offer free samples, exterminators offer free in-home inspections, health clubs offer free workouts. Customers are thus exposed to the product or service, but they are also indebted. Consumers are not the only ones who fall under the sway of reciprocity. Pharmaceutical companies spend millions of dollars every year to support medical researchers and to provide gifts to individual physicians—activities that may subtly influence investigators' findings and physicians' recommendations. A 1998 study in the *New England Journal of Medicine* found that only 37 percent of researchers who published conclusions critical of the safety of calcium channel blockers had previously received drug company support. Among those whose conclusions attested to the drugs' safety, however, the number of

Free samples carry a subtle price tag; they psychologically indebt the consumer to reciprocate. Here shoppers get complimentary tastes of a new product, green ketchup.

those who had received free trips, research funding or employment skyrocketed—to 100 percent.

Reciprocity includes more than gifts and favors; it also applies to concessions that people make to one another. For example, assume that you reject my large request, and I then make a concession to you by retreating to a smaller request. You may very well then reciprocate with a concession of your own: agreement with my lesser request. In the mid-1970s my colleagues and I conducted an experiment that clearly illustrates the dynamics of reciprocal concessions. We stopped a random sample of passersby on public walkways and asked them if they would volunteer to chaperone juvenile detention center inmates on a day trip to the zoo. As expected, very few complied, only 17 percent.

For another random sample of passersby, however, we began with an even larger request: to serve as an unpaid counselor at the center for two hours per week for the next two years. Everyone in this second sampling rejected the extreme appeal. At that point we offered them a concession. "If you can't do that," we asked, "would you chaperone a group of juvenile detention center inmates on a day trip to the zoo?" Our concession powerfully stimulated return concessions. The compliance rate nearly tripled, to 50 percent, compared with the straightforward zoo-trip request.

Consistency

In 1998 Gordon Sinclair, the owner of a well-known Chicago restaurant, was struggling with a problem that afflicts all restaurateurs. Patrons frequently reserve a table but, without notice, fail to appear. Sinclair solved the problem by asking his receptionist to change two words of what she said to callers requesting reservations. The change dropped his no-call, no-show rate from 30 to 10 percent immediately.

The two words were effective because they commissioned the force of another potent human motivation: the desire to be, and to appear, consistent. The receptionist merely modified her request from "Please call if you have to change your plans" to "Will you please call if you have to change your plans?" At that point, she politely paused and waited for a response. The wait was pivotal because it induced customers to fill the pause with a public commitment. And public commitments, even seemingly minor ones, direct future action.

In another example, Joseph Schwarzwald of

FAST FACTS
Persuasive Techniques

1 ›› Six basic tendencies of human behavior come into play in generating a positive response to a request: reciprocation, consistency, social validation, liking, authority and scarcity.

2 ›› Knowledge of these tendencies can empower consumers and citizens to make better-informed decisions about, for example, whether to purchase a product or vote for legislation.

3 ›› The six key factors are at work in various areas around the world as well, but cultural norms and traditions can modify the weight brought to bear by each factor.

Bar-Ilan University in Israel and his co-workers nearly doubled monetary contributions for the handicapped in certain neighborhoods. The key factor: two weeks before asking for contributions, they got residents to sign a petition supporting the handicapped, thus making a public commitment to that same cause.

Social Validation

On a wintry morning in the late 1960s, a man stopped on a busy New York City sidewalk and gazed skyward for 60 seconds, at nothing in particular. He did so as part of an experiment by City University of New York social psychologists Stanley Milgram, Leonard Bickman and Lawrence Berkowitz that was designed to find out what effect this action would have on passersby. Most simply detoured or brushed by; 4 percent joined the man in looking up. The experiment was then repeated with a slight change. With the modification, large numbers of pedestrians were induced to come to a halt, crowd together and peer upward.

The single alteration in the experiment incorporated the phenomenon of social validation. One fundamental way that we decide what to do in a situation is to look to what others are doing or have done there. If many individuals have decided in favor of a particular idea, we are more likely to follow, because we perceive the idea to be more correct, more valid.

Milgram, Bickman and Berkowitz introduced the influence of social validation into their street experiment simply by having five men rather than one look up at nothing. With the larger initial set of upward gazers, the percentage of New Yorkers who followed suit more than quadrupled, to 18 percent. Bigger initial sets of planted up-lookers generated an even greater response: a starter group of 15 led 40 percent of passersby to join in, nearly stopping traffic within one minute.

Taking advantage of social validation, requesters can stimulate our compliance by demonstrating (or merely implying) that others just like us have already complied. For example, a study found that a fund-raiser who showed homeowners a list of neighbors who had donated to a local charity significantly increased the frequency of contributions; the longer the list, the greater the effect. Marketers, therefore, go out of their way to inform us when their product is the largest-selling or fastest-growing of its kind, and television commercials regularly depict crowds rushing to stores to acquire the advertised item.

Less obvious, however, are the circumstances under which social validation can backfire to pro-duce the opposite of what a requester intends. An example is the understandable but potentially misguided tendency of health educators to call attention to a problem by depicting it as regrettably frequent. Information campaigns stress that alcohol and drug use is intolerably high, that adolescent suicide rates are alarming and that polluters are spoiling the environment. Although the claims are both true and well intentioned, the creators of these campaigns have missed something basic about the compliance process. Within the statement "Look at all the people who are doing this *undesirable* thing" lurks the powerful and undercutting message "Look at all the people who *are* doing this undesirable thing." Research shows that, as a consequence, many such programs boomerang, generating even more of the undesirable behavior.

For instance, a suicide intervention program administered to New Jersey teenagers informed them of the high number of teenage suicides. Health researcher David Shaffer and his colleagues at Columbia University found that participants became significantly more likely to see suicide as a potential solution to their problems. Of greater effectiveness are campaigns that honestly depict the unwanted activity as damaging despite the fact that relatively few individuals engage in it.

Liking

"Affinity," "rapport" and "affection" all describe a feeling of connection between people. But the simple word "liking" most faithfully captures the concept and has become the standard designation in the social science literature. People prefer to say yes to those they like. Consider the worldwide success of the Tupperware Corporation and its "home party" program. Through the in-home demonstration get-together, the company arranges for its customers to buy from a liked friend, the host, rather than from an unknown salesperson. So favorable has been the effect on proceeds that, according to company literature, a Tupperware party begins somewhere in the world every two seconds. In fact, 75 percent of all Tupperware parties today occur outside the individualistic U.S., in countries where group social bonding is even more important than it is here.

Of course, most commercial transactions take place beyond the homes of friends. Under these much more typical circumstances, those who wish to commission the power of liking employ tactics clustered around certain factors that research has shown to work.

Physical attractiveness can be such a tool. In a

This year Americans will produce more litter and pollution than ever before.

If you don't do something about it, who will?

Give A Hoot. Don't Pollute.

Forest Service-USDA

Social validation takes advantage of peer pressure to drive human behavior. Poorly applied, however, it can also undermine attempts to curtail deleterious activities, by pointing out their ubiquity: If everyone's doing it, why shouldn't I?

1993 study conducted by Peter H. Reingen of Arizona State University and Jerome B. Kernan, now at George Mason University, good-looking fundraisers for the American Heart Association generated nearly twice as many donations (42 versus 23 percent) as did other requesters. In the 1970s researchers Michael G. Efran and E.W.J. Patterson of the University of Toronto found that voters in Canadian federal elections gave physically attractive candidates several times as many votes as unattractive ones. Yet such voters insisted that their choices would never be influenced by something as superficial as appearance.

Similarity also can expedite the development of rapport. Salespeople often search for, or outright fabricate, a connection between themselves and their customers: "Well, no kidding, you're from Minneapolis? I went to school in Minnesota!" Fund-raisers do the same, with good results. In 1994 psychologists R. Kelly Aune of the University of Hawaii at Manoa and Michael D. Basil of the University of Denver reported research in which solicitors canvassed a college campus asking for contributions to a charity. When the phrase "I'm a student, too" was added to the requests, the amount of the donations more than doubled.

Compliments also stimulate liking, and direct salespeople are trained in the use of praise. Indeed, even inaccurate praise may be effective. Research at the University of North Carolina at Chapel Hill found that compliments produced just as much liking for the flatterer when they were untrue as when they were genuine.

(Are we then doomed to be helplessly manipulated by these principles? No.)

Cooperation is another factor that has been shown to enhance positive feelings and behavior. Salespeople, for example, often strive to be perceived by their prospects as cooperating partners. Automobile sales managers frequently cast themselves as "villains" so the salesperson can "do battle" on the customer's behalf. The gambit naturally leads to a desirable form of liking by the customer for the salesperson, which promotes sales.

Authority

Recall the man who used social validation to get large numbers of passersby to stop and stare at the sky. He might achieve the opposite effect and spur stationary strangers into motion by assuming the mantle of authority. In 1955 University of Texas at Austin researchers Monroe Lefkowitz, Robert R. Blake and Jane S. Mouton discovered that a man could increase by 350 percent the number of pedestrians who would follow him across the street against the light by changing one simple thing. Instead of casual dress, he donned markers of authority: a suit and tie.

Those touting their experience, expertise or scientific credentials may be trying to harness the power of authority: "Babies are our business, our only business," "Four out of five doctors recommend," and so on. (The author's biography on the opposite page in part serves such a purpose.) There is nothing wrong with such claims when they are real, because we usually want the opinions of true authorities. Their insights help us choose quickly and well.

The problem comes when we are subjected to phony claims. If we fail to think, as is often the case when confronted by authority symbols, we can easily be steered in the wrong direction by ersatz experts—those who merely present the aura of legitimacy. That Texas jaywalker in a suit and tie was no more an authority on crossing the street

Behold the power of authority. Certainly not lost on the National Rifle Association is that the authority inherent in such heroic figures as Moses, El Cid and Ben-Hur is linked to the actor who portrayed them, Charlton Heston.

than the rest of the pedestrians who nonetheless followed him. A highly successful ad campaign in the 1970s featured actor Robert Young proclaiming the health benefits of decaffeinated coffee. Young seems to have been able to dispense this medical opinion effectively because he represented, at the time, the nation's most famous physician. That Marcus Welby, M.D., was only a character on a TV show was less important than the appearance of authority.

Scarcity

While at Florida State University in the 1970s, psychologist Stephen West noted an odd occurrence after surveying students about the campus cafeteria cuisine: ratings of the food rose significantly from the week before, even though there had been no change in the menu, food quality or preparation. Instead the shift resulted from an announcement that because of a fire, cafeteria meals would not be available for several weeks.

This account highlights the effect of perceived scarcity on human judgment. A great deal of evidence shows that items and opportunities become more desirable to us as they become less available.

For this reason, marketers trumpet the unique benefits or the one-of-a-kind character of their offerings. It is also for this reason that they consistently engage in "limited time only" promotions or put us into competition with one another using sales campaigns based on "limited supply."

Less widely recognized is that scarcity affects the value not only of commodities but of information as well. Information that is exclusive is more persuasive. Take as evidence the dissertation data of a former student of mine, Amram Knishinsky, who owned a company that imported beef into the U.S. and sold it to supermarkets. To examine the effects of scarcity and exclusivity on compliance, he instructed his telephone sales-

Friends (who are already liked) are powerful salespeople, as Tupperware Corporation discovered. Strangers can co-opt the trappings of friendship to encourage compliance.

(The Author)

ROBERT B. CIALDINI is Regents' Professor of Psychology at Arizona State University, where he has also been named Distinguished Graduate Research Professor. He is past president of the Society of Personality and Social Psychology. Cialdini's book *Influence,* which was the result of a three-year study of the reasons why people comply with requests in everyday settings, has appeared in numerous editions and been published in nine languages. He attributes his longstanding interest in the intricacies of influence to the fact that he was raised in an entirely Italian family, in a predominantly Polish neighborhood, in a historically German city (Milwaukee), in an otherwise rural state.

people to call a randomly selected sample of customers and to make a standard request of them to purchase beef. He also instructed the salespeople to do the same with a second random sample of customers but to add that a shortage of Australian beef was anticipated, which was true, because of certain weather conditions there. The added information that Australian beef was soon to be scarce more than doubled purchases.

Finally, he had his staff call a third sample of customers, to tell them (1) about the impending shortage of Australian beef and (2) that this information came from his company's *exclusive* sources in the Australian national weather service. These customers increased their orders by more than 600 percent. They were influenced by a scarcity double whammy: not only was the beef scarce, but the information that the beef was scarce was itself scarce.

Knowledge Is Power

I think it noteworthy that many of the data presented in this article have come from studies of the practices of persuasion professionals—the marketers, advertisers, salespeople, fund-raisers and their comrades whose financial well-being de-

(Influence across Cultures)

D o the six key factors in the social influence process operate similarly across national boundaries? Yes, but with a wrinkle. The citizens of the world are human, after all, and susceptible to the fundamental tendencies that characterize all members of our species. Cultural norms, traditions and experiences can, however, modify the weight that is brought to bear by each factor.

Consider the results of a report published in 2000 by Stanford University's Michael W. Morris, Joel M. Podolny and Sheira Ariel, who studied employees of Citibank, a multinational financial corporation. The researchers selected four societies for examination: the U.S., China, Spain and Germany. They surveyed Citibank branches within each country and measured employees' willingness to comply voluntarily with a request from a co-worker for assistance with a task. Although multiple key factors could come into play, the main reason employees felt obligated to comply differed in the four nations. Each of these reasons incorporated a different fundamental principle of social influence.

Employees in the U.S. took a reciprocation-based approach to the decision to comply. They asked the question, "What has this person done for me recently?" and felt obligated to volunteer if they owed the requester a favor. Chinese employees responded primarily to authority, in the form of loyalties to those of high status within their small group. They asked, "Is this requester connected to someone in my unit, especially someone who is high-ranking?" If the answer was yes, they felt required to yield.

Spanish Citibank personnel based the deci-

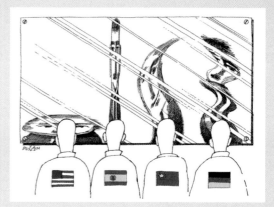

Cultural norms can alter perceptions of persuasion tactics.

sion to comply mostly on liking/friendship. They were willing to help on the basis of friendship norms that encourage faithfulness to one's friends, regardless of position or status. They asked, "Is this requester connected to my friends?" If the answer was yes, they were especially likely to want to comply.

German employees were most compelled by consistency, offering assistance in order to be consistent with the rules of the organization. They decided whether to comply by asking, "According to official regulations and categories, am I supposed to assist this requester?" If the answer was yes, they felt a strong obligation to grant the request.

In sum, although all human societies seem to play by the same set of influence rules, the weights assigned to the various rules can differ across cultures. Persuasive appeals to audiences in distinct cultures need to take such differences into account. —R.B.C.

pends on their ability to get others to say yes. A kind of natural selection operates on these people, as those who use unsuccessful tactics soon go out of business. In contrast, those using procedures that work well will survive, flourish and pass on these successful strategies [see "The Power of Memes," by Susan Blackmore; SCIENTIFIC AMERICAN, October 2000]. Thus, over time, the most effective principles of social influence will appear in the repertoires of long-standing persuasion professions. My own work indicates that those principles embody the six fundamental human tendencies examined in this article: reciprocation, consistency, social validation, liking, authority and scarcity.

From an evolutionary point of view, each of the behaviors presented would appear to have been selected for in animals, such as ourselves, that must find the best ways to survive while living in social groups. And in the vast majority of cases, these principles counsel us correctly. It usually makes great sense to repay favors, behave consistently, follow the lead of similar others, favor the requests of those we like, heed legitimate authorities and value scarce resources. Consequently, influence agents who use these principles honestly do us a favor. If an advertising agency, for instance, focused an ad campaign on the genuine weight of authoritative, scientific evidence favoring its client's headache product, all the right people would profit—the agency, the manufacturer *and* the audience. Not so, however, if the agency, finding no particular scientific merit in the pain reliever, "smuggles" the authority principle into the situation through ads featuring actors wearing white lab coats.

Are we then doomed to be helplessly manipulated by these principles? No. By understanding persuasion techniques, we can begin to recognize strategies and thus truly analyze requests and offerings. Our task must be to hold persuasion professionals accountable for the use of the six powerful motivators and to purchase their products and services, support their political proposals or donate to their causes only when they have acted truthfully in the process.

If we make this vital distinction in our dealings with practitioners of the persuasive arts, we will rarely allow ourselves be tricked into assent. Instead we will give ourselves a much better option: to be informed into saying yes. Moreover, as long as we apply the same distinction to our own attempts to influence others, we can legitimately commission the six principles. In seeking to persuade by pointing to the presence of genuine ex-

pertise, growing social validation, pertinent commitments or real opportunities for cooperation, and so on, we serve the interests of both parties and enhance the quality of the social fabric in the bargain.

Surely, someone with your splendid intellect can see the unique benefits of this article. And because you look like a helpful person who would want to share such useful information, let me make a request. Would you buy this issue of the magazine for 10 of your friends? Well, if you can't do that, would you show it to just one friend? Wait, don't answer yet. Because I genuinely like you, I'm going to throw in—at absolutely no extra cost—a set of references that you can consult to learn more about this little-known topic.

Now, will you voice your commitment to help?... Please recognize that I am pausing politely here. But while I'm waiting, I want you to feel totally assured that many others just like you will certainly consent. And I love that shirt you're wearing.

Limited offer of toys available for a short time often creates a figurative feeding frenzy at local fast-food establishments. Scarcity can be manufactured to make a commodity appear more desirable.

(Further Reading)

◆ **Bargaining for Advantage.** G. Richard Shell. Viking, 1999.
◆ **Age of Propaganda: The Everyday Use and Abuse of Persuasion.** Revised edition. A. J. Pratkanis and E. Aronson. W. H. Freeman and Company, 2001.
◆ **Influence: Science and Practice.** Fourth edition. Robert B. Cialdini. Allyn & Bacon, 2001.
◆ **The Power of Persuasion: How We're Bought and Sold.** Robert Levine. John Wiley & Sons, 2003.
◆ For regularly updated information about the social influence process, visit **www.influenceatwork.com**

Worth Publishers is pleased to announce a new line of audio resources for students *on the go!*

Psych2Go is a series of audio downloads for busy students who want to master introductory psychology "on the go." Students can use these downloads to reinforce their reading, prepare for exams, or review a concept that they find particularly difficult. Psych2Go contains the following components for each chapter of the textbook:

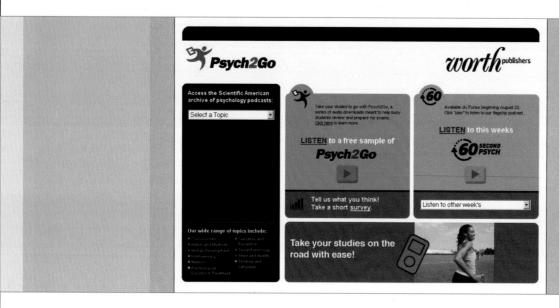

www.worthpublishers.com/psych2go

See the Frequently Asked Questions on page 2 for more information about Psych2Go.

Psych2Go Reviews Chapter summaries that convey the key concepts and themes and encourage students to think critically about the material they have read. Each review is approximately 20-25 minutes in length and contains integrated self-check questions.

Psych2Go Quizzes Comprehensive assessments that help students identify what they know well and what they need to study in more depth.

Psych2Go Flashcards Vocabulary "drills" that test students on all the key terms of a particular chapter.

The following *FREE* audio resources are also available on the *Psych2Go* site:

Produced by Scientific American exclusively for Worth Publishers, a weekly podcast covering news stories and commentaries from the world of psychology. The podcasts will be available on the Psych2Go site, and visitors can also subscribe on iTunes.

A **psychology-themed archive** of Scientific American's "60-Second Science" and "Science Talk" podcasts.